See Hear

To all children, especially Jocelyn, Sabrina & Kyrsten—M.T.
For my mum, Mary E. McLeod—C.M.

©1994 Milan Tytla (text)
©1994 Chum McLeod (art)

Designed by Brian Bean
Edited by Jonathan Bocknek

Typeset by Attic Typesetting Inc.

Annick Press Ltd.

Annick Press gratefully acknowledges the support of the Canada Council and the Ontario Arts Council.

The publisher shall not be liable for any damage which may be caused or sustained as a result of the conduct of any of the activities in this book, from not specifically following instructions or conducting the activities without proper supervision, or from ignoring the cautions contained in the text.

Canadian Cataloguing in Publication Data

Tytla, Milan
See hear
ISBN 1-55037-988-7

1. Vision - Juvenile literature. 2. Vision - Experiments - Juvenile literature.
3. Hearing - Juvenile literature. 4. Hearing - Experiments -
Juvenile literature. I. McLeod, Chum. I. Title.

QP475.7.T98 1994   j612.8'4   C94-930733-5

Distributed in Canada by:
Firefly Books Ltd.
250 Sparks Ave.
Willowdale, ON M2H 2S4

Published in the U.S.A. by Annick Press (U.S.) Ltd.
Distributed in the U.S.A. by:
Firefly Books (U.S.) Inc.
P.O. Box 1338
Ellicott Station
Buffalo, NY 14205

Printed and bound in Canada by Webcom.

See Hear

Playing with Light and Sound

written by Milan Tytla

illustrated by Chum McLeod

ANNICK PRESS LTD.
Toronto • New York

About The Author

Milan Tytla earned his Ph.D in 1982 in Experimental Psychology, specializing in vision. Since then he has been Staff Scientist in the Departments of Ophthalmology, The Hospital for Sick Children and Toronto Hospital, and taught a course in perception at the University of Toronto. Milan has been interested in perception since childhood. His first book, co-authored with Nancy Crystal, is called *You Won't Believe Your Eyes*, and is all about the visual system. His second book, *Come to Your Senses (All Eleven of Them)*, helps you discover, through simple, hands-on experiments, the many unexpected abilities you use in "making sense" of the world around you.

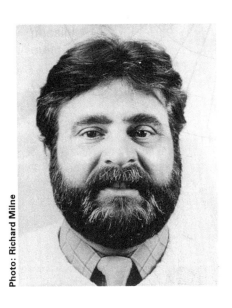

Photo: Richard Milne

About This Book

In this book you will explore your two distance senses—seeing and hearing—and the types of energy these senses pick up—light and sound. Unlike the many other senses, seeing and hearing allow you to get information about the world very quickly, over great distances.

You can read the book from front to back, or just start anywhere you choose. Whatever you do, you can have much more fun actually diving in and *doing* the experiments, especially with your friends. Most of the experiments would make excellent science projects, either on their own, or connected with other ones. You will read about some of those connections, but you can make others on your own. Most of what you need for the experiments are items you can find in your home or classroom, and in the book. But you have already brought the most complicated and important piece of apparatus: your sophisticated brain connected to your sharp eyes and ears. So . . . pick a page, explore, and have fun!

Questions?

If you have a question related to the senses of humans or other creatures that hasn't been answered by Dr. Tytla's first three books, or if you have a neat idea, unexplained observation, or comment you'd like to share, send it to him care of:

Annick Press Ltd.
15 Patricia Avenue
Willowdale, Ontario,
Canada M2M 1H9

Acknowledgements

Keith Cox, Assistant Press Supervisor, *Toronto Star*, Ontario, Canada.

Umber Manjoor, grade 11 student, Turner Benton High School, Brampton, Ontario, Canada.

Mark Simonson, Beagle Bros, Inc., San Diego, California, USA.

Dr. Martin Taylor, Defence and Civil Institute of Environmental Medicine Canada, North York, Ontario, Canada.

Chris Trumble, Firearms Examiner, Centre of Forensic Sciences, Ministry of the Solicitor General and Correctional Services, Toronto, Ontario, Canada.

Dr. Christopher Tyler, Smith-Kettlewell Eye Research Institute, San Francisco, California, USA.

Jocelyn Tytla, Joy of Music, Scarborough, Ontario, Canada.

Sandy Willis, Deaf-Blind Services, Canadian National Institute for the Blind, Toronto, Ontario, Canada.

Jim Luckett and Dr. Karen Hughes
Department of Physics. Erindale Campus
University of Toronto, Canada.

Table of Contents

Hearing
AND
Sound

THE
Sound
Chain

Frequency and Amplitude

This is the popular way to draw sound waves. The peaks represent areas of tightly packed molecules. The valleys are areas of spread-apart molecules.

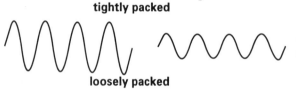

tightly packed

lower frequency and lower pitch

loosely packed

- Sound can change in frequency (FREE-kwin-see). That's how *quickly* it vibrates. Count the number of peaks in one second in the wave above. There are four. We say it has a frequency of four hertz (Hz). The wave below has a higher frequency, six hertz,

higher frequency and higher pitch

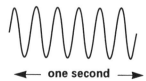

◄— one second —►

because there are six peaks in one second. If you could hear these sounds, the top one would have a lower pitch than the bottom one. Bassoons, for instance, make lower-pitched sounds than piccolos.

- Sound can change in amplitude (AM-plih-tewd). That's how *much* it vibrates. The wave above moves up and down very little, so it is not vibrating very strongly. The bottom one moves a lot. The bottom one would sound much louder than the top one.

lower amplitude and softer sound

higher amplitude and louder sound

Sound Source

All sound sources vibrate back and forth. These vibrations pack air molecules closer together when pushing forward and make them spread apart when pulling back.

Sound Waves

Sound waves are vibrations that spread out from a source like ripples in a pond. Sound waves can travel through air, as well as through other things such as water or metal. But we were designed with air in mind.

Pinna

These are the floppy, funny-looking, curly things on each side of your head. They do much more than keep your glasses from sliding off. They funnel sound into the important part of your ear. But that is not their main job.

Scientists have found that the curls help you to tell where sounds are coming from. Nobody is sure what earlobes are for, since people without them hear just fine. Maybe they are there for hanging earrings.

Tympanic Membrane

Maybe you have heard of timpani, those huge kettle drums found in symphony orchestras. That is very much

temporal lobe, just a little above each ear.) The nerve from each ear has about 50 000 individual "cables" called fibres. If the auditory nerve were somehow cut, you would be totally and permanently deaf.

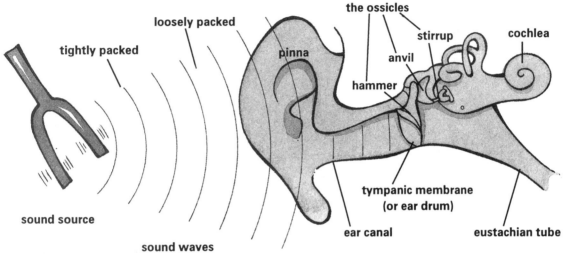

tightly packed · loosely packed · sound source · sound waves · pinna · the ossicles · anvil · stirrup · hammer · cochlea · tympanic membrane (or ear drum) · ear canal · eustachian tube

Ear Canal
There is nothing tricky here. The canal just guides sound waves to the eardrum. It does have an interesting feature, though. As you will discover later on, certain things vibrate naturally at certain frequencies. (That's called natural resonance.) It turns out that the human ear canal has a natural resonance in the same frequency range as the human voice! (Do you think this is a coincidence?) The pinna and the ear canal together are called the outer ear.

what the tympanic membrane (eardrum) is like. It is a "skin" that is tightly stretched across the ear canal. Its only job is to vibrate with the vibrations in the air. Because this is where hearing really begins, you must never poke anything into your ear. You'll never hear the same again—if at all!

Auditory Nerve
This is a thick bundle of "cables" that carry the coded signals of a sound (see Cochlea) to a part of the brain that decodes them. (That part of the brain is called the

GUESS What?

Like all of our senses, our hearing sense is as good as Mother Nature could make it. Under ideal conditions, you can hear a faint sound that causes the eardrum to move only one billionth of a centimetre. Try measuring that with your ruler!

The Ossicles

The hammer, anvil, and stirrup are the three tiniest bones (ossicles) in your body. Together they form a bridge from the eardrum to the cochlea (where the real action is). Each tiny bone is connected to the next with even tinier ligaments, and most people think that the job of the ossicles is simply to carry the vibrations from the eardrum to the cochlea. If that were true, then a single bone, instead of three fancy ones, would do the job. Mother Nature isn't that stupid! These three bones are levers, and they greatly amplify (strengthen) the incoming sound waves. (See, the problem is that the liquid in the cochlea is very difficult to vibrate. So the ossicles boost the weak vibrations from the eardrum to make waves in the cochlea.) The space between the eardrum and cochlea is called the middle ear.

The **Hammer** is connected to the back to the eardrum.

The **Anvil** is connected to the hammer.

The **Stirrup** is connected to the anvil at one end and to the cochlea at the other.

SCIENCE
Giants

Ludwig van Beethoven (1770-1827) is one of the greatest composers of all time. He created hundreds of pieces of music, including nine full symphonies! Around his 31st birthday, soon after completing only his first symphony, he noticed that he was rapidly becoming deaf. He was totally deaf by his third symphony. How did he continue to compose such brilliant music? In fact, Ludwig wrote more and better music while deaf than when not deaf. Some historians say that because of his brilliance, he could "think" music. That is, he could actually hear in his mind all the instruments playing all those notes at the same time. Others think that he actually *did* hear his music while composing by using a crafty little trick: firmly biting a stick that was pressed against the soundboard of his piano. The vibrations from the piano were carried along the stick to his skull, which in turn vibrated his cochlea. And voilá . . . sound! Unfortunately, Ludwig still couldn't hear the music from a real orchestra. Those vibrations were carried to his ears through the air and were stopped by the trouble with his middle ear. This probably explains why, after the first playing of his *Ninth Symphony,* Ludwig, with his eyes closed, continued to tap offbeat through the audience's standing ovation!

Cochlea

Welcome to the inner ear. This is the next big step in the sound chain. The cochlea (COKE-lee-uh) is a snail-shaped spiralling tunnel in your skull. It contains 15 500 hair cells that change vibrations into electrical signals the brain can understand. The diagram below shows the cochlea if it were uncurled (so you can see how it is built more easily). It is filled with fluid and is divided along its full length by the extremely flexible basilar (BAH-zih-lar) membrane. The hair cells are spread out along its length. The stirrup, on the outside, is connected to a little rubbery window so that its vibrations are passed along to the fluid. And the secret is, the basilar membrane moves in different places for different frequency vibrations. Hair cells are bent where the movement is largest, and bent cells send signals. (This is also where permanent hearing loss usually occurs. If you listen to a sound that is too loud, or for too long, the hair cells in that part of the basilar membrane become permanently damaged. Sometimes viruses can cause the same thing.)

Eustachian Tube

The middle ear is a sealed space filled with air. If the pressure outside the eardrum changes, the way it does naturally on the ground or when you fly, the eardrum stretches in or out. This can be very painful, and it affects your hearing. So, Mother Nature gave you a eustachian (you-STAY-shin) tube that connects the middle ear with your throat (around where your tonsils are). Swallowing, or a good yawn, opens the tube and air will either rush in or out to balance the pressure on both sides of the eardrum. Babies often cry on airplanes because they don't know what to do to open the tube. And people with colds and flus also have ear pain because their swollen tonsils block the tubes. An Italian doctor discovered this tube in the 1500s. His name? Bartolommeo Eustachio!

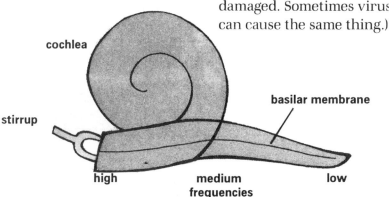

cochlea

stirrup

basilar membrane

high   medium   low
frequencies

Faster Than
A
Speeding Bullet?

Have you ever stood at one end of a race track before a race, or watched a race on TV? What happened when the starter's pistol sounded? You probably first saw the smoke from the starter's pistol, *then* the runners lunging forward, and then heard the pistol blast. This simple experience tells you that sound waves take time to travel from the source to the ear. In fact, this experience also tells you that sound travels more slowly than light. Why?

Sound waves must have a medium (molecules of "stuff" such as air or water) to carry their energy. One good way to imagine a sound wave is to picture a row of dominoes. Imagine yourself knocking the first one over and watching as each one collides with and knocks over the next. (To make this model more accurate, also imagine that each domino stands back up after being knocked over by its neighbour.) Notice that the wave moves along, but the position of each domino does not change. Sound waves travel like this, but the collisions are between molecules, not dominoes. The sound wave energy moves along as each tiny molecule collides with its neighbour, but the molecules themselves stay where they are. For sound to reach your ears, the waves must go through millions and millions of these tiny molecular collisions.

Light energy does not need collisions in order to travel. We know that because light can travel through a vacuum (where there are no molecules of stuff). In fact, that is how light gets from the sun to us here on planet Earth. Being able to travel without a medium is also one reason light can move so quickly: 300 000 kilometres per second!

Okay. So if sound is slower than light, just how fast does sound travel? Let's find out!

LET'S DO it!

Here is an experiment to help you figure out the speed of sound in air.

What You Need

string a little longer than one metre
baseball (or anything else at least that heavy)
at least one friend
large wall outdoors that produces good echoes (or a cliff face if you have one)
measuring tape
calculator (optional)
drum (optional)

What To Do

1 Glue, tape, or tie the ball (or other weight) to one end of the string. Tie a finger-sized loop in the other end so that there is exactly one metre of string between the loop and ball. You have just made a pendulum.

2 Face the wall from about 200 metres away. Have a friend with the pendulum stand in front of you and start it swinging. Your friend should stand close enough so you can see the pendulum clearly as it swings.

3 Both of you now slowly walk toward the wall.

GUESS What?

Have you ever seen movies or TV programs where the hero successfully dodges bullets? In real life, this is a super-human feat. Most bullets travel at the speed of sound (and up to 10 times faster!), and no human can react faster than about $1/10^{th}$ of a second. So, by the time your hero heard the pistol blast, or even just the click of the hammer, it would have been too late! But, of course, that's why we have super-heroes.

15

Clap your hands or beat a drum every time the pendulum reaches the end of each swing. (By the way, a one-metre pendulum takes exactly one second to swing from one side to the other, no matter how heavy the weight is.)

4 Stop as soon as your clapping sound and the echo of the previous one occur at the same time.

5 Measure your distance to the wall. Multiply that distance by two. The result is the distance the sound travelled in one second—from you, to the wall, and back to you. (To measure the distance easily and very accurately, you could use the optical rangefinder you will build on page 101.)

What did you discover? If your wall was close to sea level, and the temperature was average, you probably stopped close to 170 metres away from the wall. Let's see: 170 metres multiplied by 2 = 340 metres. This means that sound travels about 340 metres in one second. In one minute it travels 20 400 metres (340 metres × 60 seconds). And in one hour it travels 1 224 000 metres (20 400 metres × 60 minutes), or about 1200 kilometres per hour. That is very fast, but still not even close to the speed of light!

DID YOU EVER Wonder?

What is the speed limit? Well, in the nineteenth century, when locomotives had just been invented, people believed that 35 kilometres per hour was the top speed people could travel. Faster than that and you would disintegrate! Of course, we know better today as we zip along in cars and jets. In the 1940s, the new top speed was the speed of sound. Called the "sound barrier", scientists thought this was the limit. But in 1947, Captain Charles (Chuck) Yeager "broke" the sound barrier in an "eXperimental" jet called the Bell X-1. By 1960, the X-15 flew faster than 3200 kilometres per hour. Today, jet liners regularly fly at 960 — 1120 kilometres per hour. Scientists and engineers call the speed of sound "Mach 1", named after Ernst Mach who studied the speed of sound in the 1800s. Mach 2 means you are travelling at two times the speed of sound. The U.S. Space Shuttle orbits the earth at Mach 25! Today, scientists are *fairly* certain that the real speed barrier is the speed of light (300 000 kilometres per second). That's because Albert Einstein proved time slows down the faster you travel. At the speed of light, time would stop. So you could never actually reach that speed.

16

LET'S DO it!

While your hearing sense was designed to work in air, you can also hear under water. In fact, you can use this ability to see if sound travels as fast in air as in water. Let's get wet and calculate the speed of sound in water.

What You Need

a calm, quiet pond, lake or pool
at least two friends, and adults to supervise, and bathing suits for all
metal rod or pipe
hammer
stopwatch or watch with second hand

What To Do

1. Everyone into the water!

2. Have someone hold the pipe upright so it is about halfway in the water, and slowly tap the top half repeatedly with the hammer.

3. All should move as far away as possible from the tapper (and still be able to hear the tapping).

4. As the tapper continues to tap, everyone tilt your head over one shoulder and sink until one ear is under water and the other is in the air. What do you hear?

You probably heard two taps, with the one in the air reaching your ear *after* the one in the water. You have just discovered that sound waves travel faster in water than in air!

5. Now have the tapper slowly increase the speed of tapping until the tap you hear in the air occurs at the same time as the tap you hear underwater. Tell the tapper to keep tapping at that rate.

6. Ask someone to count how many taps occur in 10 seconds.

7. Divide the number of taps by 10 to calculate the number of taps in one second.

Did you find that there were four or five taps in one second? This means that

steel fence (say, 50 metres). Repeat the tapping experiment with one ear held firmly against the fence at one end and the tapper at the other. This time, the tapper will have to tap quickly with two hands, since 6000 metres per second is very fast.

Since there is no stuff in deep outer space, there is no sound. That means if you were out space-walking with a buddy and your radios broke, you couldn't talk to each other . . . or could you? (**Hint**: There *is* air in your helmet. Check out the illustration for an idea of how you might pass on a message.)

sound travels more than four times faster in water than in air. You already know that sound travels about 340 metres per second in air. That's four or five taps x 340, or around 1500 metres per second in water. Why is there a difference? As you know, sound waves need "stuff" to travel. The speed that the sound waves travel depends on two things: density (how closely packed the molecules of stuff are) and elasticity (how flexible the stuff is). Speed decreases as density increases, and speed increases as elasticity

increases. (Read that once more to keep it straight!) But water is denser than air— about eight times denser. So why is sound faster in water? It turns out that water is also much more elastic than air.

Although you might not think so, metals are extremely elastic. So, for instance, sound waves *fly* through copper at 3557 metres per second, through aluminum at 5102 metres per second, and through steel at 6000 metres per second. To check out the speed through steel, you will need a very long stretch of

Storm Tracking

You know that light travels much faster than sound—almost a million times faster. This difference probably explains why, when given a choice about *where* something might be, the brain believes the eyes more often than the ears. For instance, if you try to find a jet flying overhead, you think it is where you *see* it to be, and not where you *hear* it. Of course, that makes sense because the sound from the jet takes longer to reach your ears. (In fact, by the time you hear where it was, the jet has already moved ahead by many seconds!)

Scientists call this effect visual capture, as if the seeing sense "captured" the hearing sense. An example of visual capture that is closer to the ground is ventriloquism. Have you ever seen a ventriloquist perform? It not only *looks* as if the dummy is talking, it also *sounds* as if the dummy is talking. (Ventriloquists call this effect "throwing the voice.") Of course, dummies do not really talk, and people cannot "throw" their voices. What's happening is that ventriloquists make perfect use of visual capture. As you watch a ventriloquist perform, your brain says, "the voice must be coming from the dummy's moving lips." And that's what you hear.

Your brain also believes the eyes more often than the ears to figure out *when* something happened. This may sound like a silly question, but think about it: "Does lightning strike *when* you see the flash, or *when* you hear the thunder?" Why . . . *when* you see the flash, of course! Notice that your brain chose vision over hearing to answer the question. Let's do some more exploring with the speeds of light and sound.

LET'S DO it!

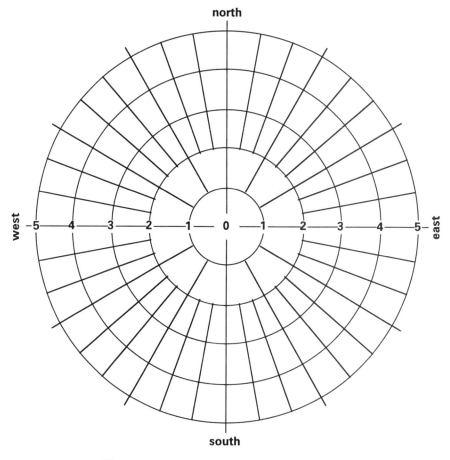

Since sound waves travel at about 1200 kilometres per hour in the air, that means sound takes about three seconds to travel one kilometre (or five seconds to travel one mile). You can use this fact to track thunderstorms.

What You Need

approaching thunderstorm (best at night)
copy of this graph (enlarged if possible)
a friend
compass
calculator (optional)
tape
pen
stopwatch (or clock or watch that counts seconds)
flashlight (optional—in case the power goes out)

What To Do

1. First, find a safe space out of the rain, on a porch or indoors, that gives the best view of the approaching storm.

2. Next, spend a little time figuring out the graph. The centre zero is your home base (where you are now). Each of the four inner circles represents the distance of one kilometre (or one mile) from the next circle. (The outermost is five kilometres—or five miles if you prefer to work with such units.) The lines (rays) spreading out from the centre point away from the home base, in different directions.

3 Find North with the compass and leave it pointing North.

4 Align this graph on a table so its North points to the North on the compass. Tape the graph firmly to a table top.

5 As soon as you see the first lightning strike, estimate its direction while your friend times how long it takes to hear the thunder. The time it takes to hear the thunder gives you a way to calculate how far away the lightning (and the storm) is. Here's how:

Delay in seconds ÷ 3 = kilometres

Delay in seconds ÷ 5 = miles

GUESS
What?

Lightning storms probably don't visit your neighbourhood very often. But around the world, about 40 000 lightning storms happen every day. At any given time, the Earth is being struck by lightning more than 100 times per second! The residents of the Tampa Bay area of Florida live in the thunderstorm capital of North America. But for some reason, the country reporting the most lightning strikes is France. (Is that because France is really more stormy than anywhere else, or because the French scientists pay more attention?)

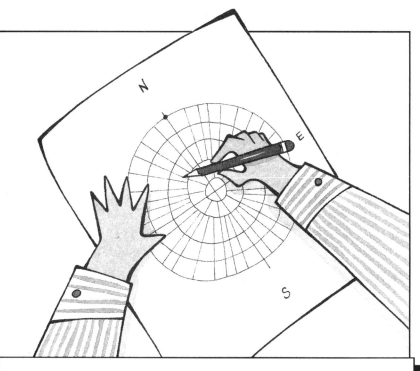

6 Mark a dot on the graph to indicate the direction that the strike occurred. Also, beside it jot down the time it occurred. For example, if the strike appeared due North and the thunder occurred 15 seconds later (five kilometres away), place a dot where the North ray crosses the outside ring. If the lightning seemed to be all around and there was no delay, place a dot in the centre. It was very close to home!

7 Keep plotting your graph until the storm has completely passed. But stay alert; it may return, or a new storm may follow! If so, change the colour of your pen to chart the new storm.

To check to see how accurate this tracking method was, compare your map with the "radar map" shown during weather reports on TV. Were they similar? It might be fun to give fresh copies of the map to several friends around town, so that you can compare notes the next time a thunderstorm passes through.

GUESS What?

If Mother Nature isn't cooperating and the weather isn't stormy, here is another "experiment" with the weather that involves sound on those hot, humid, summer days. Get close to a forest or wooded area and listen for the chirps made by a particular kind of cricket called a tree cricket. You can

use them to figure out the temperature without using a thermometer. (Remember to do the division *before* the addition.)

Number of chirps in 25 seconds ÷ 3 + 4 = °C
Number of chirps in 15 seconds + 37 = °F

Compare your calculations with a real thermometer and see how accurate your crickets are. If they are way off, chances are you have found the wrong kind of cricket. For best results, the temperature should be between 15°C and 25°C.

SOME
Shocking
Sound Experiences

The speed of sound remains fixed (stays the same) for any given temperature, altitude, and medium (the stuff the waves are travelling through). This means that extremely interesting things happen when noisy things move. Let's explore.

This diagram shows a sound source, a sports car, standing still. Its engine is idling steadily at one speed, so its sound waves spread evenly outward in all directions. And no matter where you are—in the car, or in front of it, or above it—the engine's pitch is the same. But that should not surprise you because its frequency is also the same, no matter where you are. Now, let the driver put the pedal-to-the-metal, so the car is screaming steadily along at 200 kilometres per hour, as in this diagram. The engine is still running at an even speed, but because the sound source is moving quickly forward, the waves in front "bunch-up" and become a higher frequency. The ones behind straggle and become "spaced-out" to form a lower frequency. So, if that car zoomed past you, you would first hear a high-pitched engine sound that would drop to a lower pitch the moment the car zoomed past. Notice that for the driver, the pitch does not change, because the frequency coming to the driver's ears is always the same. If you have ever heard a locomotive, motorcycle, or ambulance zoom past you, you have experienced this effect, known as the Doppler effect. But you can also create the effect yourself.

Sound waves radiate outward evenly

Porsche idling

Engine sounds the same no matter where you are

Sound waves closer at front than behind

Porsche 200 kilometres per hour

Engine sounds high-pitched as it approaches and drops as it passes

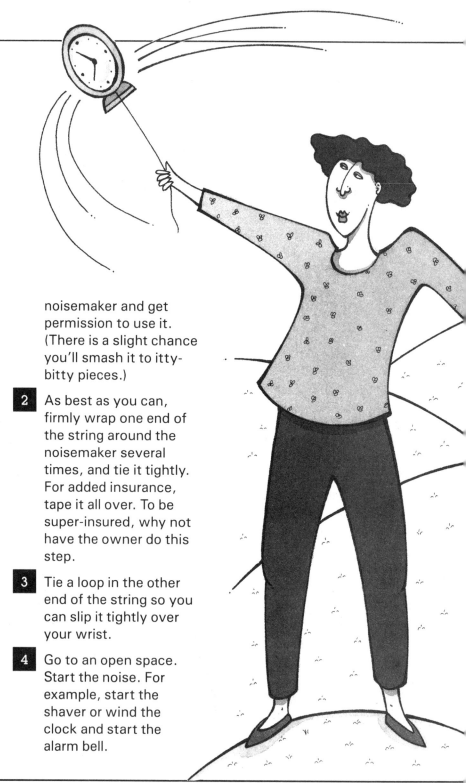

LET'S DO it!

In this experiment you can easily recreate the effect that Austrian physicist Christian J. Doppler first figured out in 1842. Fortunately, you can do the experiment without the orchestra, train, and tracks that he used!

What You Need

a friend
wide open space (preferably outdoors)
one to two metres of hefty string
strong tape
anything that will produce a loud, steady noise by itself, such as an old fashioned alarm clock or a battery-powered shaver

What To Do

1 Explain this experiment to the owner of the noisemaker and get permission to use it. (There is a slight chance you'll smash it to itty-bitty pieces.)

2 As best as you can, firmly wrap one end of the string around the noisemaker several times, and tie it tightly. For added insurance, tape it all over. To be super-insured, why not have the owner do this step.

3 Tie a loop in the other end of the string so you can slip it tightly over your wrist.

4 Go to an open space. Start the noise. For example, start the shaver or wind the clock and start the alarm bell.

5 Now, slip the loop over your wrist, firmly hold that end of the string, and steadily swing the noisemaker in a full circle above your head.

6 Listen to the pitch of the noise. Compare what you hear with what your friend hears.

7 Now have your friend do the spinning and listening.

If all went well and the noisemaker didn't fly off and disintegrate on impact, you should have experienced the Doppler effect. As the sound approached, it had a higher pitch than when it was swinging away from you. But when you stood in the middle, the pitch was steady. And you can explain why.

GUESS
What?

The Doppler effect is used by humans and other animals all around you every day. In fact, that's why Christian Doppler was so interested in it a century and a half ago. You probably know that a bat uses echoes to locate things in the dark. One way it does this is to time the delay between the chirp it makes and the return of the echo. A long delay means "far away," and a short one means "close." Some bats also listen for a Doppler effect. If the returning echo is higher in pitch than the chirp the bat produced, then that delicious bug is flying toward it. And you can guess what a lower pitch means.

Police use the Doppler effect to catch speeding drivers. Their radar guns are really transmitters and receivers of radio frequencies (way above our hearing range). Like a bat, the gun knows exactly the frequency it broadcasts, and can immediately calculate the difference in frequency between the outgoing signal and the echo returning from a car. For each speed limit, there is only one "correct" difference in frequency. The bigger the difference, the more someone is speeding. Radar guns can measure the speed of anything, such as a pitcher's pitch or a hockey player's slapshot.

You probably also know that radar is used to detect aircraft. If you send waves out into open air and there is a Doppler shift, then something is out there and it is moving. So how can high-tech military "stealth" jets be radar-invisible? It's simple, really. The sharp angles and flat surfaces *do* reflect radar, but in a direction away from the source, so the radar receiver receives no echo. Neat, eh? There are many other uses for the Doppler effect.

So far, you have been looking mostly at subsonic speeds. Those are speeds below the speed of sound. Let's move on and really speed things up. First we have to trade in our sports car for a high-tech jet. This diagram shows what happens when something noisy travels *at* the speed of sound, Mach 1. The sound that the jet engine is producing simply cannot travel any faster than the jet itself. As a result, the sound waves actually pile up in front of the jet and produce an enormously powerful single wave that would knock you over and blast out your eardrums as the jet passed—if you could stand

just to the side of the jet's path. This is the so-called "sound barrier" you read about on page 16. Of course, today we know this "barrier" can be broken and that jets can go supersonic—faster than the speed of sound. In fact, some aircraft can travel several times Mach 1. This diagram shows what happens during supersonic flight. The instant each wave is produced, it immediately falls behind the jet. The leading edges of these trailing waves add up and form a shock wave that produces what is called a sonic boom. That is the loud explosion you may have heard at air shows.

Unless you have a really spiffy jet, you cannot produce these kinds of sonic booms. But you have often heard nature's version: thunder! You may even have made some mini-sonic booms. The crack of a whip is one. The tip, when it flicks and snaps, is actually going supersonic. Even without a whip you can make a mini-sonic boom by wetting a dish towel and coiling it into a tight roll. Now flick your "whip" in your best lion-tamer fashion, and listen for the snap. That's a sonic boom. **But . . . never flick a towel or whip at anyone or any other living thing. That supersonic tip can tear out flesh!**

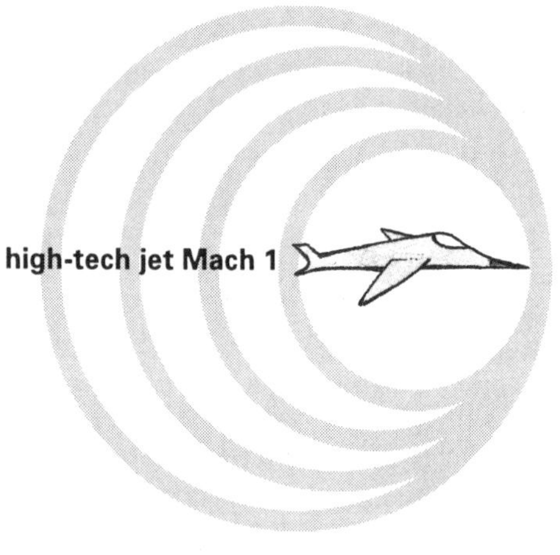

**Sound waves cannot
move forward any faster**

high-tech jet Mach 1

**Huge bang heard if you were close
to front of engine as it passed.**

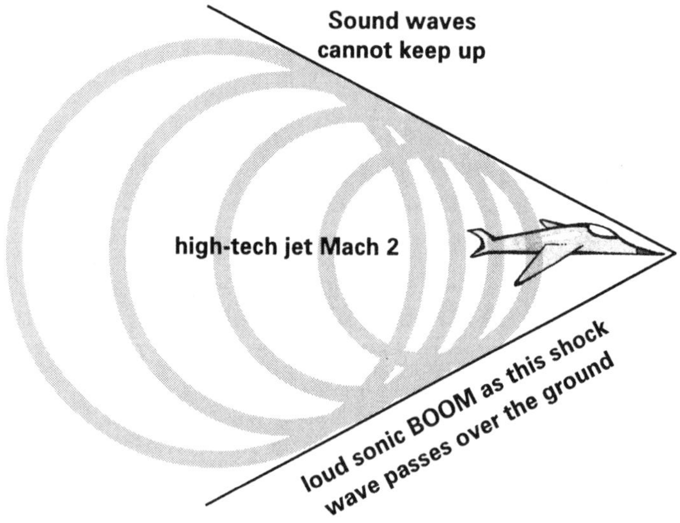

**Sound waves
cannot keep up**

high-tech jet Mach 2

loud sonic BOOM as this shock wave passes over the ground

Bouncing Airwaves

When you were calculating the speed of sound in air, you were using echoes. Echoes are the reflections of sound waves off hard surfaces. Echoes can be amusing, like the ones you produce in a canyon that has many surfaces and produces many echoes. They are also useful for animals such as bats and dolphins, which depend on echoes to locate prey and to navigate in dark or murky surroundings. Before you read about some of the technological devices humans have invented that use echoes, let's do an experiment on sound reflection.

GUESS
What?

Have you ever noticed how some blind people use their canes? A cane is an extension of the hand, so it lets them feel around places they could not touch otherwise. But you may have noticed that blind people also tap their canes repeatedly. They have learned to listen for the echoes of the taps that reflect off surfaces around them. These echoes provide a hearing "picture" of the surroundings. Blind people cannot hear any better than sighted people can.

However, blind people have learned to listen better. They have learned to hear sounds that sighted people take for granted or totally ignore.

LET'S DO it!

What You **Need**

two umbrellas (those with a
   plastic canopy work best)
clock (or watch) that ticks
string, blocks, or books
long tube (like the ones from
   wrapping paper or paper
   towels)
fairly quiet room

What To **Do**

1 Open the umbrellas and place them on the floor about two metres apart with the handles pointing toward each other.

2 Raise the handles so the shafts are level with the floor, either by hanging them from the ceiling or the underside of a table top, or by stacking blocks or books under each handle.

3 Fasten the clock to the shaft of one umbrella about 50 centimetres down from the top of the canopy.

4 Go to the second umbrella. With the tube held to your favourite ear, hold its other end at about the same place as the clock on the second umbrella. Listen carefully. Can you hear the ticking from the first umbrella?

5 If no ticking is heard, return to the first umbrella and, bit by bit, slide the clock either

28

way along the shaft. Then listen again at the same location on the second umbrella. You may also move the umbrellas closer together or find a quieter room.

6 Once you have found the ticking sound on the second umbrella, leave the clock where it is and listen at other places on the second umbrella. Can you hear the ticking at these other places?

If all went well, you discovered that the clock's ticking could only be heard at one very special point inside the umbrella. To explain why, you need to know something about parabolas. The parabola is a curve that has a very important characteristic, called a focal point. If sound waves are radiating out from the focal point, they bounce off the inside curve and travel away in parallel waves. The reverse is also true. All parallel sound waves entering the parabola reflect off the inside curve

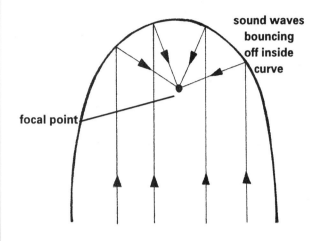

incoming sound waves

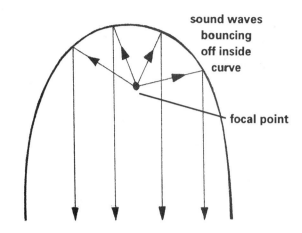

**sound waves travelling
away in parallel**

and meet at the focal point. Both facts combine to form the basis of the umbrella experiment. The clock was placed at the focus of one umbrella. The sound waves of ticking bounced off the inside canopy and travelled away in parallel, and were "received" by the other umbrella pointing at it from across the room. Your ear (actually, the end of the tube) was placed at the focal point of the second umbrella and received the concentrated sound waves. If your ear was not close to the focus, it could not receive enough waves for you to hear the ticking. (By the way, the reason you placed the tube and not your ear at the focus was

because your head would cast a large "sound shadow" and block many sound waves.)

Do you think a sound system like this one has any practical uses? Have you seen these shapes anywhere? That's right, satellite dishes. They are used to send and receive sounds over great distances. How about those parabolic microphones you see at football games or in police movies. Naturalists also use these to focus on very distant animal sounds. The microphone is at the focus of the parabolic dish.

Parabolic mirrors are also used with light. They are used to collect the sun's parallel light rays over a large

area and concentrate them at the tiny focal point. This arrangement is an efficient way to collect solar energy and can produce great heat. By collecting a great deal of light, this arrangement in the form of a reflecting telescope also allows you to see stars too dim to see otherwise. In reverse, you can find parabolic mirrors in flashlights and car headlights, where the bulb is at the focal point and rays bouncing off the mirror produce a parallel set of beams. Without the parabola, light would spread out in all directions, and weaken in a very short distance.

DID YOU EVER
Wonder?

Why are you asked to check your overcoat when you enter a theatre? Hard surfaces tend to reflect sound waves, and soft surfaces tend to absorb them. (A parabolic microphone would be quite useless if the dish were made of cloth, for example.) The reflection and absorption of sound can pose a real problem — especially for those who design concert halls. The ideal hall will absorb in the right places and reflect in others so that just about every audience member clearly and correctly hears all instruments of the orchestra. Such a hall has not been built yet, and there have been some downright disasters. When the Lincoln Center for the Performing Arts was first built, the New York Philharmonic Orchestra sounded absolutely horrible. The hall absorbed almost all the low frequencies. There were places in the audience where a single note was heard as two. And the orchestra members couldn't hear themselves or their neighbours playing! After

several renovations and a final total gutting and rebuilding costing tens of millions of dollars, most of the problems have been solved.

Another challenge to the hall designer is the change of seasons. Because of heavy clothing, a winter audience is much more absorbent than a summer crowd. (The least absorbent is an empty hall, but that would be

pointless!) In the 1960s, American scientist Walter Clement Sabine performed many experiments on sound absorption. Among other things, he found that a casually dressed adult has the same sound-absorbing effect of about seven empty seat cushions! *That* is the main reason you are asked to check your overcoat at the theatre.

Travelling
SOUND
Show

Sounds can change in their shrillness or deepness—that is, in their pitch. For instance, a piccolo produces high pitches and bassoons make low pitches. When we hear changes in pitch, it means that the sound waves coming to our ears are changing in frequency. Frequency refers to the number of waves that occur in one second. The unit for measuring frequency is called hertz (Hz for short). So,

100 Hz (waves per second) is a low frequency, and 20 000 Hz is a very high frequency. To get an idea of what different frequencies sound like, take this diagram to a standard

piano and listen to the different notes. If you can hear a "silent" dog whistle, that's 14 000 Hz, and the high squeal from inside your TV is 15 750 Hz.

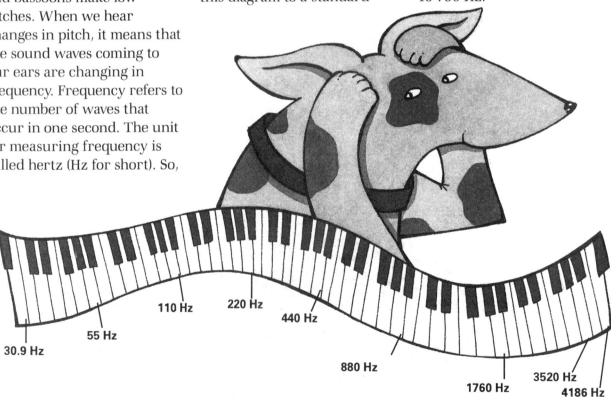

30.9 Hz

55 Hz

110 Hz

220 Hz

440 Hz

880 Hz

1760 Hz

3520 Hz

4186 Hz

LET'S DO it!

Here are two experiments to help you see how different frequencies travel. You will discover that high frequencies make good echoes and that low frequencies make good travellers.

Experiment 1

The next time you are in a large empty room such as a gymnasium or auditorium, make two short sounds with your voice: one with the highest pitch you can produce, the other with the lowest pitch. Best is to have a girl produce the high and a boy produce the low. Practise to get them the same loudness. If there is a piano in the room, use it instead. Briefly strike the highest note, then the lowest note. You will notice that the echo from the high pitch will be quite a bit louder than the echo from the low pitch. That is because the hard walls reflect the high frequency energy, but absorb most of the low frequency energy.

Experiment 2

This experiment can be done in two ways. For either way, though, you will need a good stereo system in a home or car. For best results, the stereo should be one that plays the bass sounds (very low pitch) and treble sounds (very high pitch) well.

First Method: Play a tape, CD, record, or radio that has really **BOOMY** music, with tonnes of bass. Play the music as loudly as you can stand (but first ask your favourite adult if this won't crack the loudspeakers or drive your neighbours crazy). Now try two things with the music blaring. To start with, just close all the windows and doors of the house or car, and go outside and listen. Notice that all the high pitches are barely audible (hearable) or have disappeared completely, but the **THUMP** of the bass is quite clear. That is because the walls of your house, or the glass and metal of the car, reflect the high frequencies back inside, where they bounce around until they die out. The low frequencies pass right through. Now open the windows and walk away. You will find a point where you can only hear the boomy thumping of the music. All the other higher pitches such as voices, guitars, cymbals, and snare drums are inaudible (un-hearable).

Second Method: Take a sidewalk stroll downtown or to a place where there is a lot of slow traffic. Pretty soon you will come across a car with loud, boomy music coming out of it. Notice that as the car drives away from you, or as you walk away from the car, the high pitches disappear more quickly than the bass sounds. Soon, you will only hear the boomy thumps. In other words, low frequencies travel the farthest. You might have noticed this same effect during a parade with marching bands.

Elephants can easily produce and hear sounds in the 5 to 10 Hz range. These low frequencies are such good travellers that elephants use them to communicate with each other over vast distances. Scientists only discovered this elephant communication in the 1980s. We cannot hear these frequencies because they are infrasonic—way below our hearing range (which is 20 to 20 000 Hz)—but the hair on our skin may feel it. On the other end of the scale, high frequencies make excellent echoes. That is why bats use high frequencies (up to 200 000 Hz) to locate the hard shells of delicious insects, as well as to avoid crashing into hard cave walls. We cannot hear these frequencies either, because they are ultrasonic—way above our hearing range. High frequencies are also useful because they are easy to locate. With your eyes closed you can easily point to someone else's snapping fingers. But it is very difficult to tell the source of distant, low rumbling thunder.

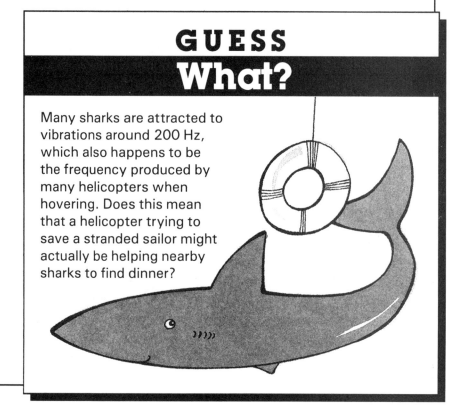

GUESS What?

Many sharks are attracted to vibrations around 200 Hz, which also happens to be the frequency produced by many helicopters when hovering. Does this mean that a helicopter trying to save a stranded sailor might actually be helping nearby sharks to find dinner?

LET'S DO it!

Just as sound waves can set your eardrum in motion, they also can cause other things to vibrate, with some interesting results. We say that the other thing is vibrating "in sympathy" with the source, or that it is resonating. Just about everything in the world has a natural resonant frequency. Let's explore a simple one.

What You Need and What To Do

1. Go to the playground with a friend, who should sit on a swing.

2. Pay attention to what you do to get your friend started and to keep swinging.

3. Notice that you cannot just push at any time. Instead you must carefully time your pushes to occur each time the swing moves away from you. So you are pushing "in sympathy" with the swing.

4. Ask your friend to "pump" to keep swinging, and observe the timing.

5. You have just discovered the swing's resonant frequency. Try pushing at other times and see what happens when you are not in sympathy.

6. Notice that you cannot change the frequency of the swing, not even by changing the weight. On this swing, an adult gorilla will swing at the exact same rate as an infant. What matters is the length of the swing. (To see if this is true, experiment by changing the length of a string attached to a weight.)

You probably found that each push of the swing did not have to be strong. Just a few, correctly timed pushes were needed. Sympathetic vibrations of all kinds are extremely important to us every day. When soldiers march in formation, they ''break step'' (walk out of step) when crossing a bridge. The bridge is certainly more than strong enough to support the soldiers, but if their steps were in sympathy with the resonant frequency of the bridge, it could vibrate and tear itself apart! In fact, something like that happened in the state of Washington. There once was a bridge over the Tacoma Narrows of Puget Sound. It was a suspension bridge (meaning that the roadway hung from cables between two posts). In 1940 the bridge was blown by gusts of wind at just the right frequency to cause it to violently twist itself apart and collapse!

Designers of cars are very interested in sympathetic vibrations. Each car has a natural resonance that can be heard when passing over bumps. Car designers try to make the resonant frequency as high as possible to produce the quietest ride.

It is also true that singers can shatter a wine glass just by singing. If your pitch matches the resonant frequency of the glass, and you can sing loudly enough, the glass will shake and shatter. (Perhaps this was the method used to cause the walls of Jericho to come tumblin' down in the Biblical story of Joshua!) To find the resonant frequency of a glass, firmly rub its rim with a moistened finger and listen to it ring. Even simpler, just tap it. It will always make that same sound. But listen to the pitch change as the glass is heated or cooled, or with different amounts of liquid in it.

Hidden Sounds:

DISCOVERING

Harmonics

Fact: Any of these musical instruments will produce a pure tone. A pure tone is one that vibrates at a single frequency. If all those instruments were playing the same note—say, the Middle C on the piano (261 Hz)—the strings, skin, and reed would be vibrating at the exact same frequency.

Question: So why do the guitar, violin, piano, kettle drum, and clarinet sound so different when they play the exact same note? Why does a guitar sound only like a guitar, and not a piano. Why does the kettle drum not sound like a clarinet?

Answer: The sound you hear is actually made up of many "hidden" sounds. These "hidden" sounds are called harmonics. Let's hunt them down.

GUESS
What?

Another reason guitars, violins, pianos, kettle drums, and clarinets sound different when playing the same note involves the way they are played. Think about how their sounds start. For instance, guitar strings are plucked, and piano strings are hammered, but violin strings are bowed (rubbed). Plucking, or striking, starts the string vibrating quickly. But bowing causes the string to start vibrating very slowly.

LET'S DO it!

What You Need and What To Do

1 Find a piano (*not* an electric model). Strike the C below middle C. (Middle C is the C in the middle of the keyboard.) It actually has many higher sounds that you can hear, but they all blend together to form the single note.

2 Gently depress middle C so that the hammer does not strike. (This lifts the felt damper off the string so it can vibrate freely.) Now sharply strike the lower C. Middle C will be ringing or resonating.

3 Repeat step 2 while gently holding down (one-at-a-time) the G, Bf, C, E, G, Bf, C keys and sharply striking the lower C. Each of these new notes should also resonate. These are the harmonics that the lower C produces on the piano. If your piano produces harmonics different from these, your lower C (and probably the whole piano) is out of tune. No problem. It just means you will have to search around using keys other than these.

4 Repeat the experiment using different sound sources playing that lower C, including a tape recording of your own voice.

You probably found that each instrument and your voice produced a different group of hidden sounds, or harmonics. They are always there and when put together give each instrument its

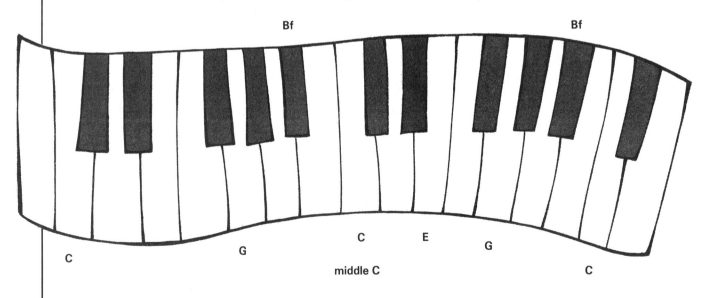

38

characteristic sound. That is why other instruments playing the exact same note still sound different—they produce different harmonics. We call this difference "timbre" (TAM-bruh). The hidden sounds come from the resonating cavity in each instrument. For instance, the piano has a box and soundboard. A clarinet has a cone-shaped tunnel. And you have cavities in the form of your throat, mouth, nose, and sinuses. These are very different from one another. So, when the string vibrates in the piano, for example, it causes the whole instrument to vibrate, and that box will produce its own special harmonics. When the reed on the clarinet vibrates at the same note as the piano, its resonating cavity will resonate at different frequencies. And when your vocal cords buzz, your resonating cavities produce still different harmonics. That is why no two voices sound exactly alike. People with "musically trained ears" can easily tell the difference between different kinds of pianos, such as a Steinway and a Bösendorf piano. In fact, theoretically,

GUESS
What?

To get an idea of how resonance works, let's do a thought experiment. Imagine sitting on a table that is vibrating. Even though your body is a unit, different parts will vibrate the most (resonate) at different frequencies. If we started with a high frequency vibration, your body hair would shake the most. As the frequency dropped, the vibration would shift to your outer earflaps, then eyeballs, then to the fingers and toes. As frequency continued to drop, your arms would shake the most, then your legs, then some internal organs and your butt and blubber (if you have any). And finally, at the lowest frequency, your whole trunk would shake.

In other words, most things will vibrate over a large range of frequencies, but there is a small range that will produce maximum vibration—resonance. Also notice that resonant frequency is related to size. Small things tend to resonate at high frequencies, while large things tend to resonate at low frequencies. You can find this throughout nature. For example, elephants are huge and have huge basilar membranes, and can only hear in the low frequency range. Bats are small (some are smaller than an elephant's basilar membrane!) and can only hear high frequencies.

two pianos from the same maker should not sound *exactly* alike.

Imagine listening to an orchestra. Now think about the thousands of frequencies and harmonics from the different instruments and voices that are dancing along your basilar membranes and in your brain. Yet, you can easily pick out and listen to a single instrument. *How does your brain do it?* It's easy actually. Over time, it has learned the kinds of harmonics a particular instrument makes. All the harmonics belonging to one instrument will start and stop at the exact same time. Your brain can pick out these "packages" of sound.

GUESS What?

Male mosquitoes are attracted to females by the beating of their wings. So that they don't confuse the sexes, females beat at about 500 Hz and males beat at a slightly higher frequency. This fact was discovered purely by accident (as are many scientific facts). In the late 1800s, a row of electric lights was installed for the first time on a hotel in New York City. Swarms of male mosquitoes were drawn to the lights, because they misread the humming of the lights as females!

Siren Song

While talking with a male friend, gently place your fingers on either side of, and just above, his Adam's apple and feel the vibrations coming from the vocal cords. They are being "stroked" by passing breath in much the same way a bow strokes a violin string. A good apparatus for feeling how vibrations cause sound waves is your own stereo system. Turn it on to a normal level of loudness and place your hand in front of the speaker. Find where the vibrations are the strongest. You should be able to feel the difference between loud and soft sounds. You might also feel the difference between different frequencies. If you are a keen observer, you might notice that your skin feels the lower frequencies, and the hair on the back of your hand feels the higher frequencies. Get permission to remove the cover from the speaker (if it comes off easily). You can actually see the speaker cone vibrate back and forth in the lower frequency range. Get permission to lay the speaker on its back, and gently pour a little uncooked rice or barley onto the speaker's cone. (This is harmless.) Watch the grains dance as the speaker vibrates Experiment making sounds with other household things. For example:

- gently twang a fork gripped between your teeth and try different sized forks;

- pluck an elastic and stretch it by different amounts;

- blow across the top of a bottle and add different amounts of water.

In each case you created vibrations in the air to produce a sound. Come to your own conclusions on how the changes in each case changed the pitch. In the meantime, let's make a siren.

LET'S DO it!

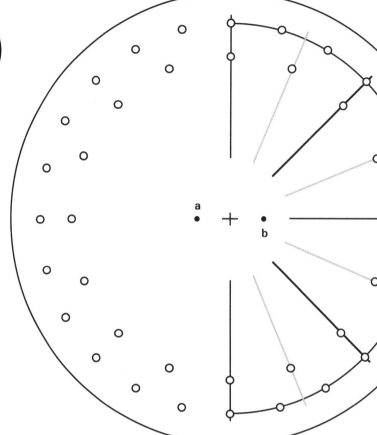

What You Need

a friend
photocopy or tracing of this disc
single-hole punch (shape doesn't matter)
one metre of string (not thread)
push pins and cutting board
scissors
drinking straw
scrap of stiff flat cardboard (such as Bristol board or heavier)

What To Do

1 Put the copy of the disc over the cardboard, and pin both onto the cutting board in four places outside the disc. Firmly and carefully trace the disc outline onto the cardboard so that you leave a dent.

Push a pin through each of the dots, including **a** and **b**. (For now, totally ignore all other lines.) Unpin the copy and cardboard.

2 Cut the outside circle out of the cardboard, and punch out all the pinholes except **a** and **b**. For **a** and **b**, use a sharp pencil to make holes just big enough for the string to pass snugly

through. It is most important that the circle be as round as possible and that holes **a** and **b** are in exactly the correct positions.

3 Feed the string through hole **a**, then through **b**, and tie the ends together. Slide the disc to the middle.

4 Hook your forefingers through the loops at each end and grasp the string with your thumbs. Have your friend wind the disc at least 20 times.

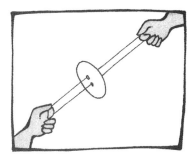

5 Now start the disc spinning by gently tugging then releasing the string repeatedly. Once you get the hang of it, the disc should spin rapidly. (If your disc wobbles too much, your timing might be off, but more likely your disc is not round enough, or holes **a** and **b** are in the wrong place.)

6 With the disc spinning, ask your friend to blow through the outside circle of holes with the straw. Repeat with the inside circle.

7 Listen to the pitch of your siren as your friend changes circles and as the disc speeds up and slows down.

Your siren raises two interesting questions. First, why does it make any sound at all? Well, you know that there must be vibrating air. In this case, the vibrations are set up by the disc as its spinning repeatedly blocks and unblocks the air coming out the straw. This produces waves of packed and unpacked air molecules.

Second, why is the pitch different between the two circles of holes, or when the speed changes? Because frequency is changing. Look at the disc. Starting at the 12 o'clock position, count the number of holes in each of the two circles. The outside has 24 and the inside has only 16. So, for any steady speed, the outside circle will produce a higher frequency (24 vibrations per revolution) than the inside (16 vibrations per revolution).

When the disc speeds up, the holes pass the straw more rapidly, and the frequency rises. (So does the pitch.) And when the disc slows down . . . well, you can figure it out.

Try making your own discs and predict how they will sound. For example, give the left half a higher frequency than the right half. (This is what the extra lines are for.) Repeat the instructions, but now, on the left half of the disc, only punch out the holes on the outside circle. On the right half, only punch out where the *black* rays from the centre cross the line of the outside circle. What should this sound like? Now punch out where *all* the rays cross the outside circle, then listen. What happens if the holes have fuzzy edges—like those made with a pencil and not a punch?

Humming

TO THE

Beat

In the experiment on page 38, you found out how harmonics combine to produce unique sounds. Harmonics are usually far apart in frequency. What happens when two frequencies come very close to each other? Well, they interact in weird and interesting ways. Let's find out how.

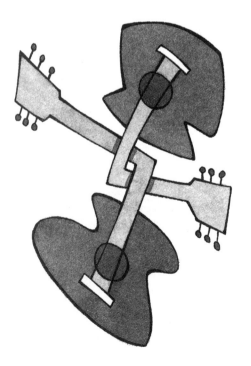

DID YOU EVER
Wonder?

Why can't we hear an infinite range of frequencies? The simple answer is that frequencies beyond our 20 Hz to 20 000 Hz range just do not contain much information for humans. And there are other reasons. Our high frequency hearing is first limited by our size. The basilar membrane cannot vibrate infinitely quickly. As newborns, a few of us could hear up to 40 000 Hz. But soon after birth that upper limit drops quickly. Scientists have discovered that the rate of loss at the high frequencies is around 160 Hz every year after the age of 40, and it speeds up after that. The reason for

this loss seems to be a gradual stiffening of the ossicles, and a loss of hair cells. At low frequencies, there should be no such problem, and it looks like Mother Nature built in this lower limit.

In a very quiet room, plug your ears with your baby fingers and listen. You have blocked out waves coming from the air. That low rumbling you hear is coming from your muscles and joints, and you might also be able to hear the thud of your pulse. It looks like humans were designed to normally filter out these distracting noises the body makes.

LET'S DO it!

What You Need

two similar simple
  instruments, such as
  guitars, recorders, or other
  band instruments (two
  people who can sing or
  whistle and hold a steady
  note will also work)
a friend
stopwatch or a watch with a
  hand that counts seconds

What To Do

1 If you are using
someone else's
instruments, ask if you
are allowed to change
their tuning, and find
out how. (It's very
simple.)

2 Adjust the instruments
so they are way out of
tune.

3 Play a middle-of-the-
range note on one
instrument and have
your friend copy that
note by re-tuning the
other instrument. Try to
keep the loudness of
the two instruments the
same.

4 Listen carefully to the
two notes. Sometimes
you will hear two totally
separate notes.
Sometimes you will
hear one note doing
something weird. And
at other times you will
hear only one pure
note.

As you probably discovered, when the two notes were far apart, you heard two notes. And when they were exactly the same, you heard only one. But *when the notes got close to each other,* you heard one note warbling or beating. Repeat the experiment, and when you get steady beats, use the stopwatch to count the number of beats that occur in 10 seconds. Then divide by 10 to get the number of beats in one second. So, if you counted 20 beats in ten seconds, the beat frequency was two beats per second. That number is interesting because it is the exact .

difference between the two frequencies. For example, if your note was 500 Hz, your friend's note was either 498 or 502 Hz. This diagram shows how the beats occur. On the top is the wave produced by the 500 Hz note by itself, and below it is the wave from the slightly faster (and higher) 502 Hz note. In the air, the waves will be combined. Peaks will add and troughs will subtract, leaving the slightly more complicated wave at the bottom that beats two times per second. You have seen this happen if you have watched ocean waves bounce off a breakwater. As

a reflected wave passes an incoming wave, sometimes the two peaks unite to make a super-peak; and when troughs cross, they produce a super-trough. You could try this out in the bathtub. With your forearm, make slow waves and watch the way they add (super-wave) and subtract (super-trough).

Beats are very useful. When an orchestra is tuning-up before a performance, the members all tune to the first oboe and listen for beats between it and their own instruments. Piano tuners also use beats when adjusting the strings of a piano.

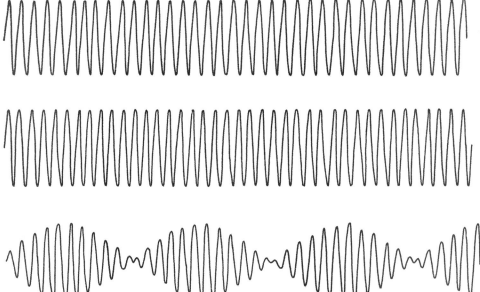

wave produced by a 500 Hz tone

wave produced by a 502 Hz tone

the two waves combined

GUESS
What?

What do you think would happen if you had two identical sound sources but you arranged them so that the peaks of one occurred exactly when the troughs of the other did? That's right — you would have complete silence. The two sources should totally cancel each other out. In fact, you already know this! When you push *with* the swing, it goes higher and higher. But, if you push exactly *opposite* to the swing, it will quickly stop. That is the thinking behind a new "electronic muffler" designed by Noise Cancellation Technologies Incorporated.

Cars without mufflers are extremely loud. The job of standard mufflers is to bounce the exhaust gas around until most of the energy is "used up" and the roar is muffled.

Unfortunately, such mufflers are not the best solution. They rust, need to be replaced every few years, and rob the engine of a lot of power. Electronic mufflers should last forever, cost about as much as one muffler, and leave the power

untouched. The *idea* of an electronic muffler is really quite simple. It listens to the sound with a microphone, then produces an upside-down copy of it. Therefore, the sound source is totally silenced. Some day we may have sneaky helicopters, ships, and subs that are capable of real "silent running!" But as scientist Martin Taylor of Defence and Civil Institute of Environmental Medicine Canada points out, this kind of noise-cancelling has at least two major problems. First, low frequencies are

easily cancelled, but high frequencies are almost impossible. So, for example, it would be easy to cancel the thump-thump-thump of a helicopter's motor, but extremely hard to cover the swooshing high frequencies that come from the blades. Second, to work perfectly, the cancelling signal must come from the exact same place as the source. Looking at the helicopter again, a great deal of the noise comes from the blade tips. Now *that's* a difficult problem to solve.

Body Talk

Have you made any sounds lately? In fact, we humans make a great deal of sound and noise with our bodies. We speak to pass on information, and sing and play instruments mainly for pleasure. We construct machines and vehicles that make the most deafening sounds. And sometimes, just for the fun of it, we just make a racket! These activities have a purpose and are mainly under our control. But our bodies also produce other sounds that we have much less control over. Let's see . . .

Sneezes & Coughs

Europeans in the 1600s believed that sneezes "cleared the mind." Therefore, someone who sneezed a lot was thought to be truly important and intelligent. Scientists now know that a sneeze is the body's attempt to clear particles and other junk (like dust, pollen, or boogers) from the nose. A sneeze is serious stuff. Its spray can travel at 200 km/h. *That's hurricane force!* Soon after that, the droplets evaporate, leaving the germs to float in the air.

English-speakers agree that a sneeze sounds like *AH-CHOO*. The *AH* part occurs while inhaling, and the *CHOO* part expresses the violent exhalation. People who speak other languages have different expressions for the sound of a sneeze. Here are a few examples:

French: *Atchoum*
Greek: *Apsou*
Hungarian: *Hapchee*
Japanese: *Hakufhon*
Korean: *Etchee*
Pakistani: *Echink*

GESUNDHEIT!!!

A cough is very similar to a sneeze, except now the irritation is in the throat or lungs. The rough sound comes from the air rapidly blasting past your vocal cords. Notice that you do not cough out the nose. It's as if Mother Nature said, "Send that junk out the mouth, so the particles won't start a sneezing fit." The force of the cough can be so strong that your eyeballs jiggle in their sockets and affect your vision (see page 90).

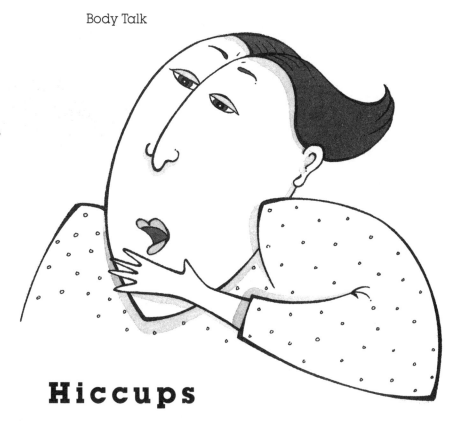

Hiccups

Hiccups are really weird! Scientists still do not understand why we get them, but they do understand what they are. Right underneath your lungs, around the bottom of your ribcage, there is a muscular membrane called the diaphragm (DIE-uh-fram). It completely divides your chest cavity from your

abdomen. When the diaphragm tenses up, it pulls on the lungs which then fill with air. As the diaphragm relaxes, it pushes the air out. That's right—that steady rhythm is called breathing, something that will continue for the rest of your life. But once in a while, your diaphragm begins a series of uncontrollable jerks or snaps called spasms. These spasms cause the lungs to quickly suck in a huge amount of air that slams into your epiglottis (eh-pih-GLAW-tis). That's the "hic" sound. (By the way, the epiglottis is the valve in your throat which normally stops

food from "going down the wrong way.")

Hiccups usually disappear on their own. However, before then you can become pretty tired because of the unusual, long exercise. But imagine, there are people who have steadily hiccupped for over 30 years! Just as odd are the kinds of different remedies people have for getting rid of hiccups. Ask around and see how many "cures" you can find and try them out the next time you get the hiccups. (My favourite is to plug your ears and take 10 gulps from a glass of ice water that someone else is holding for you.)

Snores

Snoring has puzzled scientists for centuries. The snoring itself is simple to understand. During sleep, many parts of the mouth and throat are relaxed and flap around while you breathe. The uvula (YOU-view-lah)—the "punching-bag" hanging down in the back of the mouth—is one of them. But is snoring accidental or is there a purpose to making that thunderous roaring noise during sleep? Let's look at some facts and see if you can come up with the same answer that Carol Anderson Travis did. She's a paleoanthropologist (PAY-lee-o-an-thruh-PAUL-o-jist)—someone who studies (*ologist*) ancient (*paleo*) humans (*anthropo*). The facts are:

- Many more men snore than do women.
- Men have louder and deeper voices than women.
- Snoring occurs during the deepest part of sleep.
- During deep sleep the mind is "disconnected" from the senses and muscles (so you don't hurt yourself, for instance, during a dream).
- So, sleeping out in the open, the way early humans did, is really dangerous, because

you wouldn't know if a lion, tiger, or bear was about to gobble you up (and you couldn't do much about it anyway).

Do you have an answer? Dr. Travis thinks that snoring is "left over" from those early times. By making loud roaring-like sounds (snores) during sleep, your slumbering group is signalling, "We are awake and dangerous, and there are many of us!" Of course, this may not be the best or only reason for snoring. It is just a theory—an idea that helps explain known facts. But if you remember that Mother Nature rarely makes mistakes, and is never wasteful, this is a darn good explanation for a really strange behaviour.

Yawns

When you are tired or bored, your breathing and your heart rate slow down. That means your body parts (including your brain) are getting less oxygen than when you were alert. Notice that you also usually yawn when you are tired or bored. Scientists think that the big gulp of air you take during a yawn is an "oxygen jolt" to get you back up and running. There is no *need* to make that loud sigh when you exhale. It probably just feels good. The weird part is that scientists do not understand why watching someone else yawn often makes you yawn. It also happens in the rest of the animal kingdom. In fact, you can make someone yawn with a hand puppet whose mouth you can open wide! Try it and see (adding your own sound effects). Nobody knows for certain why Mother Nature put this into our design, but she must have had a good reason. Can you think of one?

GUESS What?

You may recall from way back on page 12 that the hammer, anvil, and stirrup are connected to each other and these bones move very freely. They also have tiny muscles attached to them that can tense up and really limit their motion. When they do, you become temporarily deafened. This is called the acoustic (ah-COO-stick) reflex and you can experience it during a very strong yawn. Scientists are not sure why we have it. They used to think it was there to prevent the hair cells from being damaged by very loud sounds such as thunder. But this idea doesn't really work. A loud sound would first have to get to the hair cells to trigger the reflex, but by that time the damage would have been done. The current idea is that the reflex is there to hush the sounds we make when eating or talking. This idea came from a report that the reflex also occurs every time you move your jaw.

Borborygmi

Have you ever been somewhere quiet, such as a library or auditorium, only to hear your stomach growl and squeak in a most embarrassingly loud way? The medical name for those gurgles, pops, and grumbles is borborygmus (bore-bore-RIG-muss). A bunch of them are called borborygmi. Most people think the growling comes from your stomach when it is empty. That's partially incorrect for two reasons. First, the sound more often comes from your intestines. And second, borborygmi can happen any time. Your stomach is a super-strong muscular bag. When it is empty (and you are hungry), there is a lot of air and a little liquid that sloshes around and gurgles. But after you have eaten, your stomach goes to work squeezing, churning, and mashing the food into mush. Then the food is squirted into your five metres of intestine, where it goes on a roller-coaster ride of more churning, squooshing, and squirting, and all kinds of interesting sounds are made. By the end of that ride, the intestines have extracted all the nutrients from the mush and you are left with . . . you know . . . poop!

Burps

In some countries, burping or belching is considered rude. But there are places around the world where if you don't belch after a meal, you have insulted the cook and the host. Usually you can control a burp so it is very quiet. But if you are caught by surprise, the air can make a bellowing *BRAAAAAP* sound as it races past your vocal cords. Where does that air come from, and how did it get there? Have you noticed that after eating some foods, you almost always burp? Soda pop is one of these and provides a big clue. We all normally have quite a bit of air and other gases in our stomachs, and it gets there each time we eat. Sit back and think about food. Ice cream and whipped cream are filled with bubbles. All baked goods are, too. You gulp a lot of air when you drink or eat anything. And the fizz in soda pop comes from a gas injected into the liquid. The more you eat and drink, the more gas collects in the stomach until it can't hold any more. So you burp.

Have you ever seen the explosive fountain that

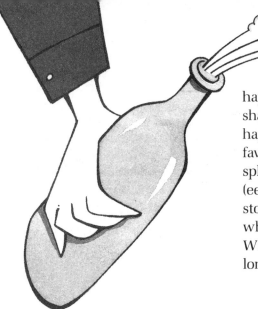

happens when soda pop is shaken? That is exactly what happens when you gulp your favourite soda. The pop splashes down your esophagus (ee-SOFF-ah-gis) and into your stomach, releasing lots of gas which then escapes as a burp. With other foods it takes longer. Babies have to be burped, not because they don't know how, but because they spend so much time lying flat on their backs. In that position the mush in the stomach blocks the esophagus, and they can't burp the gas. Over time the gas buildup becomes painful. See if you ever burp in that position.

Exhaust

When gas escapes out the top end of our digestive tract we call it a burp. When it escapes out the other end it's called a . . . let's call it a *traf*. Everyone trafs—even your principal, teacher, the Prime Minister, President, and the Queen. In fact, some scientists think the typical healthy adult trafs up to 10 and maybe 20 times a day.

Trafs have been given a huge variety of names: SBD (silent but deadly), fart, breezer, toot, and fluff are only a few (or is that "aphew"?). Medically, a traf is called flatus. And to find out who traffed we ask: "who cut the cheese?" or "who broke wind?" or "who passed gas?"

Trafs are pockets of gas that escape from the intestines. Like burps, some of that gas comes from the air you swallow while eating and drinking. But more is actually created in the intestines by microscopic organisms called bacteria. They help your body break down food and they produce gases along the way. Soon too much gas builds up and has to be released out the only available exit—the anal sphincter (AY-nul SVINK-ter). The sound of the traf depends on the amount of gas and the looseness of the sphincter muscle. To get an idea, inflate a balloon and let the air escape as you stretch the neck between your fingers by different amounts. Listen to how the sound changes as you change the balloon's sphincter (opening) and as you squeeze the balloon.

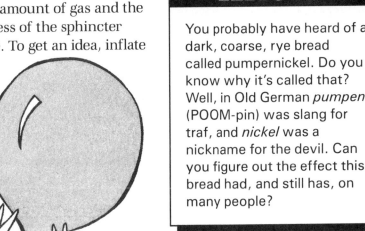

DID YOU Know?

You probably have heard of a dark, coarse, rye bread called pumpernickel. Do you know why it's called that? Well, in Old German *pumpen* (POOM-pin) was slang for traf, and *nickel* was a nickname for the devil. Can you figure out the effect this bread had, and still has, on many people?

Whether or not a traf is smelly depends on what you eat. Cabbages, onions, and beans produce the smelliest, sulphur-smelling trafs in most people. That's really not surprising because these foods contain a lot of sulphur, and the bacteria release it.

By the way, the bacteria in your intestines are called *Escherichia coli* (esh-ehr-RISH-ee-ah COLE-eye), or *E. coli* for short. They make up almost one half of your poop. That's very useful information, because to see if water (or anything else) has been polluted by human waste, scientists just have to see if the number of *E. coli* in a sample of water is above the acceptable limit. That's certainly easier (and a lot less icky) than looking for the real thing!

GUESS What?

There's a popular camping rhyme that goes:
Beans, beans, the musical fruit,
the more you eat, the more you toot,
the more you toot, the better you feel.
Makes you want another meal!
So, why *do* beans make you "musically toot?" Mainly because each bean is wrapped in a tough cellulose cover that is *extremely* difficult to break down! (Maybe you've noticed that corn passes through you almost unchanged. The kernels are totally wrapped in cellulose!) So, as your intestines and *E. coli* whistle while they work, so do you! Incidentally, contrary to the rhyme, the *more* (often) you eat, the *less* you toot, because your intestines and *E. coli* get used to doing the work.

Light

AND

Sight

THOSE
Energetic
Little Photons

Light

Anything that is visible must either make light or reflect it. The sun and light bulbs are examples of light sources, and the moon and this page are examples of reflectors.

Scientists still are not sure what light is, but most agree to talk about it as if it is made up of tiny, energetic particles called photons. These photons zip along at 300 000 kilometres per second. While moving, photons also vibrate. So, a photon makes a wavy path as it moves. Some photons are very energetic and vibrate quickly. When they enter the eye we see blue. Other photons vibrate more slowly. We see them as red. All the other photons, and colours, fall in between these two to form the visible light spectrum. You have seen this spectrum if you have witnessed a rainbow.

Contrary to popular belief, light rays do not always travel in straight lines. But they try to. Rays can be bounced off shiny surfaces (see Reflection and Colour). Their path can also be bent by travelling through stuff (see Refraction). Very strong magnetic fields and gravity can also bend light. (That's how astronomers often see distant stars that they know must be covered by a closer star. The gravity of the closer star bends the light from the distant star, making it visible. It's like peeking around a corner.)

Reflection and Colour

It is important to realize that light rays or photons themselves are not really coloured. Neither are the surfaces of objects. Colour is

A SIMPLE
Problem

Photons travel 300 000 kilometres per second, and it takes around eight minutes for sunlight to reach the Earth. How far are we from the Sun?

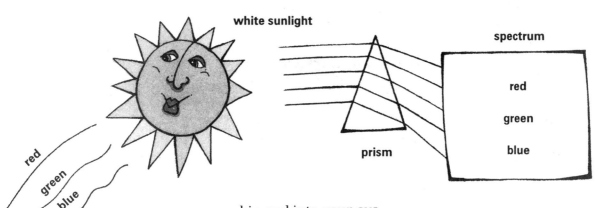

white sunlight

spectrum

red

green

blue

prism

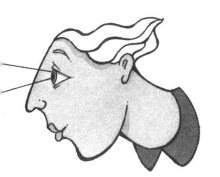

seen when a type of photon hits a type of cell in the eye called a cone. But to make things easy, we can talk about "red, green, or blue" light (photons), and "red, green, or blue" cones.

A red apple looks red because its skin absorbs all the photons except the red ones. They bounce (reflect) off the skin and into your eye, striking all the cells there. But only the red cones will become excited and signal to the brain, "red apple." Black surfaces appear black because they absorb all the photons, whereas white ones reflect all the photons. That's why black cars are hotter than white ones. Absorbed photons produce heat. On a hot summer day, leave a black and a white piece of paper in full sunlight for 30 minutes. Then feel them.

Refraction

Light bends when it passes from one kind of transparent stuff to another, such as from air to water, or from air to glass. This bending is called refraction. You have seen refraction at work many times. For example, a pencil looks bent when it is leaning in a glass of water. The rainbow you see after a rainstorm or in

GUESS What?

Until plastics were invented, glass was the material used to make prisms and lenses. And even though glass looks like a solid, it is not! Glass is not exactly a liquid either, but instead behaves like a super-thick syrup. Scientists call this kind of stuff an "amorphous (ay-MORE-fuss) solid". This just means that glass is a solid without shape, something between a solid and a liquid. So, in your lifetime, your bedroom window will not change its shape noticeably. But it will deform if you press it firmly and steadily for the next few decades. There are ancient windows around that really are thicker at the bottom than at the top because of this slow flow over the centuries.

the spray of a garden sprinkler is also caused by refraction. The colour spectrum in rainbows is especially interesting.

During the 1600s, Sir Isaac Newton played with prisms a lot. A prism is a wedge of glass. When light passes through, it is refracted, and the direction of bending is toward the base. The interesting thing is that if you start out with white sunlight, a beautiful coloured spectrum comes out. Rainbows occur because water droplets act just like tiny prisms. Newton did not discover the spectrum. (It has been seen in rainbows and crystals for thousands of years.) But he was the first to suggest that white light was a mix of all these colours.

The more energetic the photon, the more it is refracted. Blue is bent the most, and red the least. Now you know why the sky is blue. As sunlight streams through our atmosphere, the energetic blue photons are scattered and refracted the most. Red morning and evening skies occur because the sunlight is coming from different angles and passes through more atmosphere, so only the red photons make it to your eye.

Focus

A lens is any transparent material with at least one curved surface. The light rays coming from an object are refracted by the front and back surfaces of the lens to form an image. In the eye, when that image falls on the retina, it is in sharp focus. If the retina were closer to or farther from the lens, the image would be blurry.

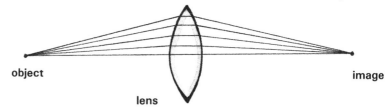

object   image

lens

GUESS What?

In 1989 the United States sent the Hubble Space Telescope into orbit. It is a reflecting telescope with a highly polished mirror. If you have read page 29, you probably guessed that this mirror is a parabola that collects a great deal of light from very distant, dim stars and brings that light into sharp focus to be sent back to Earth. The purpose of the Hubble was to observe the universe from outside the distorting effects of Earth's atmosphere. Without any "light pollution" from cities, the pictures should have been absolutely fantastic. To the scientists' surprise, the pictures came back only a tiny bit better than those taken from Earth. It turns out that the mirror was not curved enough (oops!). Around the edge it was off by 1/100th of the thickness of a human hair. Not all the light rays crossed the focal point; this left a blurred circle. The Hubble was myopic (shortsighted)! The mirror cannot be replaced, but in December of 1993, space shuttle astronauts installed a telephone-booth-sized set of "glasses" into the telescope to correct the myopia. Watch the news to see how successful the glasses are.

Your Window
ON THE
World

Cornea

Close your eyes, roll them around, and use your fingers to feel that bump moving under your lids. That's your cornea. The cornea is mostly water and is a transparent part of your sclera. The cornea also acts as a lens, and it actually does most of the bending of light to form an image on the back of the eye. (The actual lens does the fine tuning.) Look closely at a friend's cornea. You shouldn't find a single vein or artery. So, how does the cornea stay alive? Read about the aqueous humour. Why are there no blood vessels? Read about the fovea.

Lens

The job of the lens is to change its thickness to bring things into focus on the retina. It

fattens for near things and relaxes for far. The name "lens" comes from the Latin word for lentils, which have the same shape. The lens is made of transparent layers, like an onion. With age, the lens yellows and becomes stiffer. That's why many people need glasses to help them focus later in life. A

cloudiness of the lens due to injury or disease is called a cataract.

Aqueous Humour

Aqueous humour means "watery liquid" in Latin. Lying right behind the cornea, it is constantly renewed (pumped and drained) and keeps the cornea alive by supplying oxygen and food and removing waste. This "tap" and "drain" usually work perfectly. But in a few of us as we get older, the drain becomes clogged or too much aqueous comes out of the tap. The pressure slowly builds, leading to a form of blindness called glaucoma. Fortunately, most glaucomas are preventable.

Iris and Pupil

The iris is the coloured, circular muscle behind the cornea. The pupil is the hole left by the iris. It shrinks as more light enters the eye. Your pupil also tells other people how alert you are. When you are tired or bored it can be very small, and when you are excited it can open up wide. Can you now guess why gamblers often wear dark sunglasses, and what "cues" some so-called psychics use to figure out what's going on inside your head?

Sclera

The sclera is the tough leathery outer layer, "the whites of your eyes". If the sclera is pierced, the eye will deflate just like a balloon, but is much more difficult to fix.

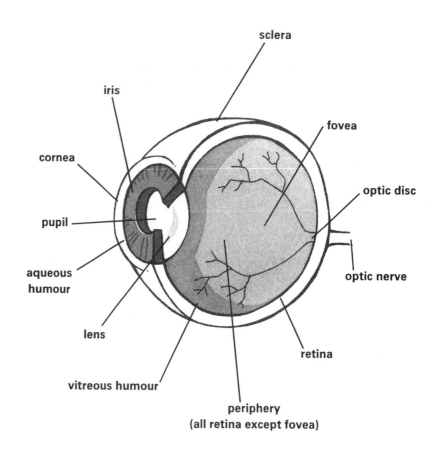

periphery
(all retina except fovea)

Vitreous Humour

Vitreous humour means "glassy liquid" in Latin, but it is really a crystal-clear jelly that keeps the eyeball inflated. Unlike the aqueous, the vitreous is not renewed. Throughout your life, chunks of retina and other stuff become loose and float around, casting permanent shadows on the retina. They are called "floaters." Don't worry—floaters are perfectly normal (unless they seriously block your vision).

Retina

The retina is an extremely fine mesh of nerve cells lining the inside. It processes the image for the brain, and means "net" in Latin. The 128 million photoreceptors in each eye change lightness and darkness into electrical impulses, and many additional cells change these impulses into a code the brain understands. The retina has been called the "film" of the eye. But the most advanced video system does not even come close.

Rods and Cones

Our eyes have two different types of photoreceptor: rods and cones. Rods are rod-shaped and, yes, cones are cone-shaped. *(This is one time scientists didn't make up goofy labels for body parts!)* Both types change light energy into electrical signals that ultimately reach the brain, but that is where their resemblance ends. Rods are "colourblind", see best at night, and only live in the periphery. Cones only "see" colour, are nightblind, and are concentrated in the fovea. Humans have three types of cones.

Most nocturnal (night-time) creatures have only rods, and many birds, and some lizards and amphibians have only cones. Can you guess what each critter can and cannot see?

Fovea

This is a part of the retina that only creatures with forward-pointing eyes have. Later on you will discover why. You use your fovea when you "look at" something. You turn your eye so that the image of what interests you falls on it. Of all the places on the retina, the fovea is best at seeing fine detail and colour. Note there are no blood vessels here (for the same reason there aren't any in the cornea, aqueous, lens, and vitreous), so there is nothing in the way of forming the best image possible.

Periphery

The periphery is the part of the retina surrounding the fovea. You use it to see "where" something is. For example, out of the "corner of your eye" (periphery) you detect this tiny creature scrambling by. So you turn your eye to see "what" it is (with your fovea). As you travel deeper into the periphery, colour vision disappears and your ability to see detail drops sharply, but your ability to see motion is at its best.

Optic Disc

This is where one million cables leave the eyeball and the veins and arteries enter. It's a pretty boring place except for the fact that, because there's so much traffic here, there's no room for photoreceptors. In other words, you are totally blind here. (You might be tempted to call this the "blind spot", as most books do. Strictly speaking, that's wrong: the blind spot is a spot out in your visual world; the optic disc is a place in your eye!) You can find your "blind spot" using the next page. Close your right eye and with your left eye stare at the little apple from at least 40 centimetres away. Now slowly come forward and stop when the big apple disappears. Don't peek to the left, or the big apple will reappear because you have moved your optic disc. If the big apple doesn't completely disappear, keep your eye on the little apple and gently twist the book clockwise or counter-clockwise to find your blind spot. Then turn the book upside down and find the blind spot in your right eye.

Optic Nerve

This is a huge bundle of one million mini-cables that carry information about an image from the eye to the brain. Most people think the eyes do the "seeing", but seeing really happens in the brain.

Image Formation

These are just two of the millions of light rays reflecting off the apple to the eye. Together, the cornea and lens bring them into focus on the retina to form a tiny upside down image of the apple. Why don't we see the world upside down? The brain flips it right-side up.

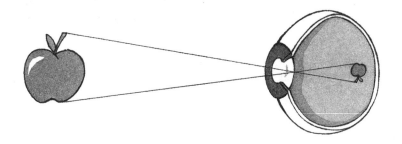

Amazing Greys

The eye is designed to form an image of the world on the retina. And it is the retina's job to turn that image into signals the brain can understand. You already know what the *brain* sees. In fact, you are watching it at work *right now*. (Sit back, look around, and think about it.) But what does the *retina* see? In other words, what does the retina look for, to send to the brain? Scientists are not yet sure, but they have a good idea. One thing seems certain. There is no way the brain can handle all of the signals coming in from every single rod and cone at the same time. (Actually, as you will soon see, it doesn't have to.) Perhaps you have figured that out already. In each eye there are *128 million* photoreceptors (rods and cones), but only *one million* fibres ("cables") leave the eye through the optic nerve! So, the retina sends only the most critical information to the brain.

This whole book is filled with line drawings—cartoons of people and things drawn using only lines. You have no trouble understanding what they mean. Look at this one. Do you recognize him? If not, flip back to the photo at the beginning of the book to refresh your memory. It's me. Now carefully compare the photo with the cartoon. They're not really close at all.

In fact, the real world has very few cartoon lines! But notice that the lines in the cartoon version of me fall in the same place where there are edges in the photo. (Edges occur where a light area meets a dark area.) Does the retina hunt for edges? What if . . . *just what if* the retina exaggerated what it thought were edges?

In the late 1800s, an Austrian named Ernst Mach

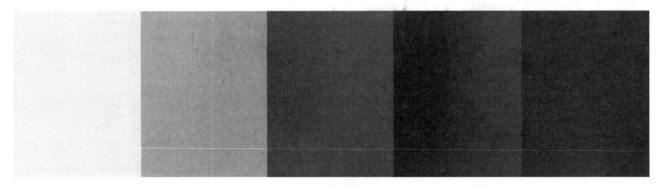

Mach bands

was one of the first scientists to show that this is probably true. (Yes, that's right—the same Mach who studied sound.) He studied diagrams like this "staircase." In each step, the greyness is exactly the same. But if you look closely at an edge where a lighter step touches a darker one, you should see bands on either side. The darker step seems to get darker closer to the edge, and the lighter one seems to get lighter closer to the edge. These are called Mach bands. (To prove to yourself that they are not really there, pick one step, cover its neighbours and the edges with thick paper, and watch the bands disappear.) To Mach, this meant that the signals coming from rods and cones do not go directly to the brain. Instead, they interact to *exaggerate* the edge. Mach correctly thought that this interaction happens in the

retina. But that was not proven until *50 years later!*

So, the rule is: light areas make dark areas seem even darker, and dark areas make light areas seem even lighter.

Let's watch this rule at work. The greyness of the two smaller centre circles is exactly the same. (Prove it by covering the picture with paper that has had two holes cut out so that only the centres can be seen.) But the smaller circle surrounded by dark seems much lighter than the other one. Notice also that,

unlike the Mach bands, the whole area is affected, and not just the edges. That's probably because the grey circles are totally surrounded.

The "trick" on the next page is even neater. Think of it as the grid of a city. The lines are streets that cross at intersections. Just pay attention to the top left for now, where the streets are white and the blocks are black. You might begin to notice a ghostly darkening at the intersections only. It's all in your eyes. Cover everything

but one street, and the spots disappear. Now think about the rule. The streets are surrounded by more black than the intersections. So, they are lightened more than the intersections. On the bottom right, you will see light spots at the black intersections. Use the rule to figure out why. This drawing is called the Hermann Grid, named after a 19th century German scientist who studied the effect. This is one time it is okay to see spots!

Hermann grid

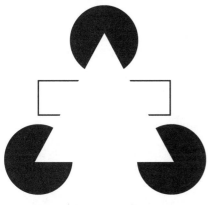

Kanizsa's triangle

Here is another effect that is especially interesting, and scientists still do not have a complete explanation for it. If you are like most people, you probably see a very white triangle lying on top of three discs and a rectangle. The triangle probably seems whiter than the surrounding paper. Believe it or not, the

triangle simply does not exist (at least not on the paper). You are making it up. This effect probably starts in the retina. The blackness of the discs lightens the white in their pie-shaped mouths which then spreads toward the others. But the sharpness and straightness of the triangle's sides could not be created in the retina. Scientists think this stage must be happening in the brain, partly because only the brain has the ability to detect shape. Although this effect was first

described in the early 1900s, and probably was experienced much earlier than that, an Italian scientist in the 1950s worked on it a lot. That is why this triangle is usually called Kanizsa's Triangle. Try to make some different ones using different shapes.

ONLY THE
Shadow
Knows

It is extremely important that your brain knows how far away things are from you and from each other. Right now, pick up something close to you, such as a pencil. Notice how quickly you did that, and that you probably didn't miss. Obviously, your brain is very good at judging distance. But how does your brain do it? Think for a minute. To pick up that pencil, your brain had to know *exactly* where it was in the three dimensions of space—width (left/right), height (up/down), and depth (near/far). Figuring out the pencil's place in the first two dimensions, width and height, is easy. The retina already has those two dimensions. But how do you calculate the third dimension, depth, if you have retinas that see only two dimensions? The

secret is that your brain is *extremely* crafty. It has many ways to figure out that third dimension. Later on, you will explore the brain's best method—using two eyes. Even with just one eye, though, the brain is very good at guessing distance. But, of course, you already knew that. Paintings and TV can be very realistic,

and give the impression of depth. Yet paper, canvas, and the TV screen only have the two dimensions of height and width!

Close one eye and casually look around. You can easily tell which objects are in front of others, and you can guess how far away different things are from you. Now, think

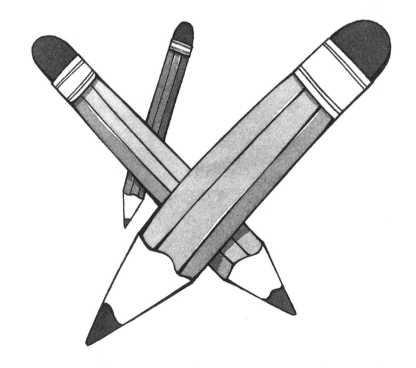

"clue" to distance. You know this is a perfectly flat drawing, but it seems to have real depth. Some of the circles seem to bump out of the page. Others seem to be hollowed-out dishes. Yet they were all made the same way. Each is just a circle that goes from near-white on one side to near-black on the opposite side. The only difference is that some are light at the top, while others are dark at the top.

Have you figured out what your mind is doing? Since light almost always comes from above, if something is bright on top and dark on the bottom (as if in a shadow), it must stick out toward you. If it is dark at the top and bright at the bottom, it must be dented away from you. Now turn the page upside down and watch the dishes turn to bumps and the bumps to dishes right before your eyes! By the way, this change proves that the dishes and bumps are in your mind and not on the page. Turn the page only halfway around, so that the shading is left to right. The circles will flip in depth, because now the brain is not sure which way is up, and does not know which one to choose. Obviously, shading is a very powerful and important clue to depth.

about how you do this. Let's see . . . if one thing covers another, then the first thing must be in front of the other. If pebbles on a beach look progressively smaller, they are probably farther away. And as you look at railway tracks in the distance, the retina says they are getting closer and closer, but your brain knows they are parallel. So they must

be off in the distance. Your brain knows these and many other rules about distance. A very powerful one involves shading.

Point to the sun or the moon. In fact, point to any light source. Most, if not all, are above you. In other words, light almost always comes from above. Your brain knows this and uses it as another

How Keen Are You?

If you have ever been to visit an eye doctor, you have probably seen a chart like the one on page 69, only larger. It is used to measure your acuity—how fine your vision is. Try it! Look at this chart from one metre away in full sunlight. The doctor would say your acuity is okay if you could read down to line nine, the second line from the bottom. If you wear glasses, take them off and see how far down you get. Also try each eye separately. See if each is different from the other and if either one is worse than both

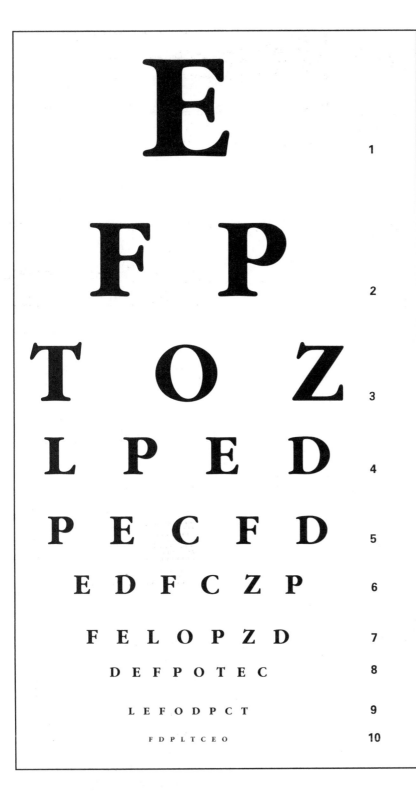

together. Two eyes often really *are* better than one!

One thing that really affects your acuity is the amount of light around you. The darker it gets, the worse your acuity becomes. You can easily test this out for yourself. Look at the chart again and record the line number of the smallest letters you can read:

- in full daylight,
- in a room at night with one dim light far away from the chart,
- and in the middle of the night with only starlight coming through your window.

Make sure the chart is always *one metre* away.

Acuity also depends very much on which part of the retina you use. Acuity is best at the fovea (the part of the retina you use to look *at* things), and gets steadily worse as you look away (in the periphery). See this for yourself by doing the test again in full daylight. This time, though, do not look directly at the letters. Instead, read them out of the "corner" of your eye by looking at the right edge of the chart, beyond the numbers. It's hard, but try your best not to peek. You might only get down to line six. (By the way, a few people have lost the fovea because of disease, and this is about as well as they can see). Try it again, but now focus about a hand's-width to the right of the chart's edge. You may only be able to see the top E.

DID YOU EVER
Wonder?

What does 20/20 vision mean? Maybe you have noticed that the doctor's large-scale eye chart is usually way down at the other end of the office. In fact, it is 20 feet from the chair where you sit. (This distance is good for testing because your eye, and especially your lens, is fully relaxed.) The sizes of the letters on the 20/20 line (line nine on *our* small-scale chart) were chosen so that they are the smallest size that can be read comfortably from 20 feet away by most adults with normal vision. So, if you can see at 20 feet what all other "normals" can see at 20 feet, you have 20/20 vision. That is called normal. If your acuity were very poor, say 20/400, that means you can see at 20 feet what "normals" can see at *400 feet!* (Instead of

moving the chart that far away, scientists simply chose to magnify the letters. For example, the top letter of most charts is 20/200, which can be read by "normals" from 200 feet away.)

An acuity of 20/400 may sound terrible, but guess what— that is roughly how poor your acuity was when you were born. Can you figure out what 20/15 or 20/10 means? (**Hint:** If you can read the *bottom* line of our chart, you have 20/15 acuity!)

Eye doctors are switching to the metric way of expressing acuity. Six metres is very close to 20 feet. So, can you guess what "normal" metric acuity is? That's right—6/6. Is an acuity of 6/120 good or bad? (**Hint:** That's the acuity you were born with.)

Starlight, Starbright

As you discovered, your fovea has the highest (best) acuity. It can see the tiniest detail. The photoreceptors in the centre of the fovea, cones, are very skinny and packed tightly together. So, the brain can easily detect tiny separations between details, like the branches of a tiny "E" on an eye chart, for example. Out in the periphery, the photoreceptors, rods, are fatter and aren't packed as closely as in the fovea. So, when the brain "looks out" the periphery, details have to be much farther apart to be seen as separate. And as you discovered, your periphery could only see the larger letters on the eye chart. You can test this idea another way by looking directly at your fingertip. (You are using your fovea when you do this.) You should be able to see the tiny grooves of your fingerprints. Now keep looking in the same direction (forward), but swing your hand out to the side where you can just barely see it (in the extreme periphery). You can find a place where you cannot even count the number of fingers!

To get an idea of what the brain is faced with, here are pictures taken with a computer "eye" whose photoreceptors' sizes can be adjusted. The top picture is the actual image of two Es from an eye chart. The middle picture shows the computer's-eye-view when adjusted to have skinny, tightly-packed photoreceptors, as in your own fovea. (Take a look with a magnifying glass to see the tiny dots clearly.) Both the large and small Es can be

E **E** **actual picture**

E **E** **computer picture using skinny dots (fovea)**

E **computer picture using fat dots (periphery)**

easily seen. But see what happens with fat photoreceptors—that's what is happening in the bottom picture. The large E is fairly easy to see, but the small E could be just about anything. This is what your brain sees out your periphery.

71

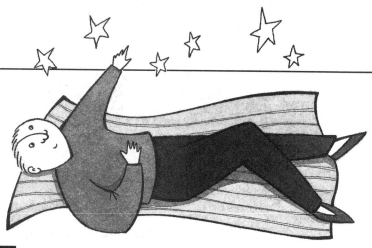

LET'S DO it!

Just because your periphery has lousy acuity doesn't mean it is useless. Let's discover one of the many ways the periphery is "better" than the fovea.

What You **Need**

family and friends
cloudless night sky filled with stars (get out of the city if you can)
comfy blanket
flashlight (to read these instructions)

What To **Do**

1 Lie on your back on the blanket and stare up at the night sky. Let yourself adjust to the dark (10 to 20 minutes).

2 Carefully look around for a star that is barely visible out of the "corner" of your eye. (In other words, use your periphery.)

3 Now look *directly* at the same star—in other words, use your fovea. If the star is dim enough, it will have disappeared! To see it, you will have to look just off the fovea.

4 Hunt around for other stars. (For fun, also look around for orbiting satellites. They are usually easy to find.)

You just discovered an effect known to astronomers for centuries. You cannot have good night vision and good acuity in the same place on the retina. Instead, one is traded for the other. Your periphery has excellent night vision and easily picked out the dim star. But when you swung your eye around to put the star on your fovea, it disappeared because there wasn't enough light for your fovea to see. In fact, the very centre of your fovea, where acuity is the absolute best, is totally nightblind! So, to see dim stars, you have to use the part of your retina just outside the fovea, which has enough acuity to see tiny stars and has enough sensitivity to pick up their dim glow.

Try to imagine what is happening in the brain when the light is very dim—when few photons are falling on the retina. Cones and rods differ in their sensitivity to light. The fovea is very unlikely to "capture" the few photons raining down on it because cones need to be struck by many photons before they signal. However, the periphery is very likely to capture a photon because any rod will signal if struck by only one photon.

Do
THE
Jerk

If you can read close to the bottom line of the eye chart, your vision is called normal. You would also be able to see each of *60* super-skinny pairs of black and white stripes packed into the width of your baby fingernail held at arm's length. These are measures of visual acuity—the finest detail that you can see. Most other animals can't see nearly so finely. The acuity of cats, or human babies, for example, is only one-tenth that of human adults. This means they could see only six pairs of fat stripes on that fingernail. And a goldfish would only see about two really fat stripes in that same space. Anything finer has no detail, and looks no different from a smooth grey. A cat, goldfish, or human baby definitely cannot read an eye chart or tell you whether or not they see stripes! *So how do we know what their acuities are?*

GUESS
What?

When measuring visual acuity, doctors have to be very careful of what the patient is actually doing. There is a story of a child who first read the eye chart from top to bottom with her right eye closed, and then with her left eye closed. Then she asked the doctor if she should read the chart with *both eyes closed!* And she could. Obviously, she had memorized the chart. That's why doctors often skip lines here and there, and sometimes ask you to read the line backwards.

LET'S DO it!

Vision scientists have come up with several clever ways to measure acuity. One way uses an eye movement that you cannot easily control, called OptoKinetic Nystagmus (OKN). That is a mouthful but its meaning is really simple: jerky eye movements (nystagmus) caused by visual (opto) movement (kinetic). Let's experience OKN.

What You Need

a friend
photocopy or tracing of this stripe pattern
black, fat markers, or paint, and a pencil and ruler
strip of three pages of white typing paper taped end-to-end (or computer paper)

What To Do

1 Lay your long strip of paper lengthwise.

Position the stripe-pattern bar lengthwise on the strip of paper in the upper left corner. Make a pencil mark where each black bar starts and ends. Repeat, sliding the stripe pattern along the strip of paper until you have marked its full length.

2 Repeat step one on the bottom length of the strip.

3 Use the ruler and marker to join the pencil marks on each side of the strip, so that you have black, parallel lines running vertically (up and down) across the strip. Blacken the area between the lines where each black bar should be. Use the stripe pattern as a guide.

4 Now hold your strip up so that the black lines are vertical. Start with one end held about 25 centimetres from your friend's face.

5 With your friend looking straight ahead, start moving the strip sideways and watch for

OKN. Repeat, trying different speeds, and be sure your friend looks at the middle of the strip, not toward the top or bottom. Too fast or too slow, or too high or too low, and the eyes won't move. Also, encourage your friend to keep the page in focus.

Did you see the OKN? Most of us have experienced OKN when in a train or subway entering or leaving the station. Your eyes rapidly, uncontrollably jerk left and right as you look out the window for your waiting friend or the name of the station. Your eyes are trying to keep up with the visual flow. If there is no flow or if the moving pattern is invisible, *there's no OKN. And that's the secret!* If the cat's or baby's eyes are doing OKN when the stripes move, then they must be able to see the stripes. But if their eyes keep still when the stripes move, these stripes must be invisible to them.

Mixed-Up Colours

In your retina, there are about 120 million rods and about 8 million cones. Cones are concentrated at the fovea, whereas rods are everywhere else. In the extreme periphery there are no cones. And in the very centre of the fovea, there are no rods. Because rods and cones work very differently, your vision is different in various places on the retina. For example, rods have nothing to do with colour vision, so your extreme periphery is colourblind. (Check it out. While staring straight ahead, move a brightly coloured object to the side until you can barely see it. You can find a place where you can just see the object, but you cannot tell its colour.) And as you discovered earlier, the very centre of your fovea is nightblind.

Cones have everything to do with colour vision. Humans have three kinds of cones. Some become most excited when struck by "red" photons. Others are activated best by "green" photons. And still others respond best to "blue" photons. But if we have only three types of cones, how can we see all the colours in the rainbow? The short answer is that the brain knows how to mix colours.

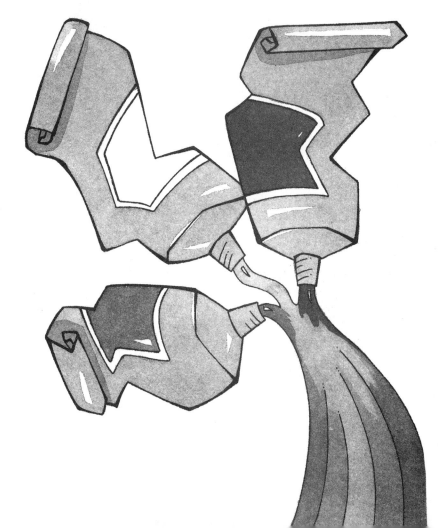

LET'S DO it!

With just a few things you can learn everything you would ever want to know about colour mixture in the brain. (This isn't the only way to mix coloured light. It's just one simple way, and the procedure is very close to the one used to make the siren earlier, on page 42.)

What You Need

a friend
photocopy or tracing of this disc
one metre of string (not thread)
push pins and cutting board
scissors
scrap of stiff flat cardboard (such as Bristol board or heavier)
coloured pens, markers, or paints

What To Do

1 Put the copy of the disc over the cardboard, and pin both onto the cutting board in four places outside the disc. Firmly and carefully trace the disc outline and the dotted lines onto the cardboard so that you leave a dent. Push a pin through each of the dots at **a** and **b**. Unpin the copy and cardboard.

2 Cut the outside circle out of the cardboard. Use a sharp pencil to make holes at **a** and **b** just big enough for the string to pass snugly through. It is most important that the circle be as round as possible and that holes

a and **b** are in their correct positions.

3 Colour each of the three pie sections so that one is red, one green, and one blue. The order doesn't matter.

4 Feed the string through hole **a**, then through **b**, and tie the ends together. Slide the disc to the middle.

5 Hook your forefingers through the loops at each end and grasp the string with your thumbs. Have your friend wind the disc at least 20 times.

6 Now start the disc spinning by gently tugging and releasing the string repeatedly. Once you get the hang of it, the disc should spin rapidly. (If your disc wobbles too much, your timing might be off, but more likely your disc isn't round enough or holes **a** and **b** are in the wrong place.) This effect works best with the fastest spin.

What happened to the colours? If all went well, they blended into a shade of white. But that wouldn't happen if you mixed the paints or inks together. Try it. Mix the same markers or paints on a piece of paper, and you get, well . . . dark mud! So what's happening? Well, it turns out that mixing light (which your spinner did) is different from mixing paints or inks. Think about paint. Red paint absorbs all but red photons. Green paint absorbs all but green photons. And blue paint absorbs all but blue photons. So when you mix these paints, each colour absorbs the few photons that the other colours reflect. The end result is that very few photons are reflected at all! The disc, however, reflected all three types of photons. Spinning it blurred the different colours, so that each part of your retina got all three coloured lights. Your brain said, "If my red, green, and blue cones are excited, white light must be falling on my retina."

How can you see yellow without yellow cones? It turns out that red and green cones can also "see" yellow photons. So if the red and

GUESS
What?

Not all creatures have the same number or kind of cones that we have. In fact, not all humans do. Some people are born missing one or two types. (More often they are not missing, but are damaged.) Such people are referred to as colour blind, but strictly speaking most are colour-deficient. If, for instance, you had a problem with your red cones, you would have trouble telling the difference between ripe and unripe tomatoes. Colour deficiencies are extremely rare in females, but affect one in eight males.

Many creatures that roam the deeper oceans have mostly blue cones and some cones sensitive to ultraviolet. (Ultraviolet photons are even more energetic than blue and are invisible to us.) Other freshwater fish, like the piranha and goldfish, have mostly red cones and some sensitive to infrared. (Infrared photons are less energetic than red; they are also invisible to us).

Many creatures create their own light. Fireflies, for example, create their own chemical light to attract the opposite sex. Some fishes, octopi, and jellyfish that live on the ocean floor do the same to light up their dark worlds. But most interesting is the bottom-dwelling fish called pachystomias (pack-ee-STOME-ee-us) that produces red light which is invisible to almost all its prey. But pachystomias has red cones which *can* see that light and allow it to zero in on its meal.

green cones are equally excited, the brain says "yellow!" Try it and see. Make another disc, but this time colour the top half red and the bottom half green. Give it a spin and see.

This kind of colour mixing is around you everywhere. Get a magnifying glass and zoom in on the coloured dots of a colour TV. You will see only three: red, green, and blue. Compare a yellow with a white area and see which dots are lit up the most. Magnify a printed coloured page of a magazine. There are those dots again. In the case of TV and printing, the dots are blurred because they are too small to be seen clearly at your normal viewing distance. The TV, movie, and printing industries are very lucky that our brains can make up all the colours by mixing just three. Otherwise, thousands of pigments would be needed! And most of us just wouldn't be able to afford such a TV or movie, or even a single printed page. Try spinning discs with other colours on each half, and work out other colour mixes.

GUESS What?

You can think of a lens as two prisms attached at their bases, and smoothed out. Think about what else you know about prisms. Since blue photons are refracted more than red, if white light is coming from the object, shouldn't there be many differently coloured images of the object, with the bluest one closest to the lens and the reddest one the farthest? Well, actually they *are* there, but they aren't visible in everyday seeing. Try this simple experiment.

Find a stereo or video system with those tiny, brightly coloured lights. In a very dark room, you will notice that when the red light is in focus, the green or blue ones aren't. And the opposite is true. What you are doing is changing your focus to place these different images on the retina. When one is in focus, the other has to be out of focus. The next time you see a slide show, look closely at a black-and-white edge. You should see a blurry rainbow. The lenses in most slide projectors aren't corrected for this colour problem, but the lenses in expensive cameras are. That's one reason they are so expensive.

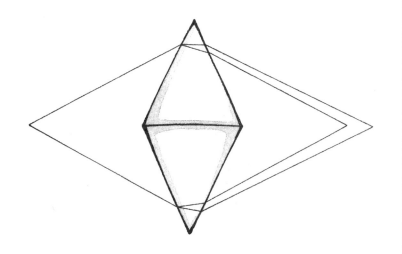

Freezing Action

et's begin by asking what sounds like a silly question. How does your brain know that something is moving? As the image of a moving thing slides across the retina, it is exciting neighbouring rods and cones in order and in one direction. The brain monitors that order and figures out that something is moving in a certain direction. There is nothing tricky here. But have you seen old Western movies in which the spoked wheels of a moving wagon seemed to be moving too slowly, rotating backwards, or even sometimes standing still? If you haven't, look for it. The effect is really weird. Another place to see this effect is on the wheels of real cars on a real highway at night (but not during the day). How can this be? We know the wheels must be rolling forward. So this must be some kind of illusion. In fact, you might have already guessed that, because there is no real motion in movies. It is all an illusion. Let's find out what's happening. Or as we usually say . . .

LET'S DO it!

In this project, you will build a simple apparatus and do four experiments that explain this effect. Among other things, you'll see your forward-spinning bike wheel turn backwards, and watch water travel back up into the tap. You are going to build an apparatus that looks like this. So, let's go!

What You Need

friends (including an adult to cut and to help design)
long, hefty plastic straw (like the ones from hamburger stands)
very bright flashlight (with fresh batteries) or a projector
a cardboard tube (to fit snugly over the flashlight or projector lens)
hand drill (or variable-speed electric drill)
drill bit, dowel, or pencil that fits snugly into the straw
tape (wide adhesive or duct tape is best)
flat bristol board or light cardboard at least 40 cm × 40 cm*
cardboard box with the top removed (about 40 cm × 40 cm on the front, and about 24 cm deep*)
ruler, pencil, tack, and string
Xacto knife
a room that can be made pitch black
black paint and white paint (optional)
*Note: The bristol board and the front of the box can be larger than 40 cm × 40 cm, as long as they are the same size. Also, the box has to be large enough for the drill to fit inside.

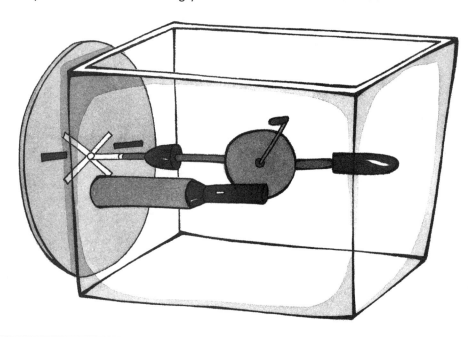

What To **Do**

1 You are going to cut a circle out of the bristol board which is about two centimetres smaller than the front of the box. Find the centre of the bristol board by drawing two lines connecting the opposite corners.

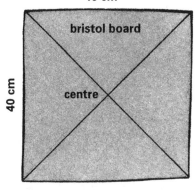

40 cm

bristol board

40 cm

centre

2 Tie one end of a string to a pencil. Push the tack through the string so the tack is 19 cm away from the pencil. (If your box is different from 40 cm × 40 cm, measure the height or width — whichever is shorter — divide that by two and subtract one centimetre. That's how far *your* tack should be from the pencil.) Pin the

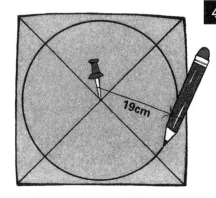

19cm

tack to the centre and, with the string tight, draw a circle. Cut out the circle.

3 On the circle, draw two rectangles that are eight centimetres tall by one centimetre wide. Position the rectangles along one of the lines so they are on each side of the centre. Each must be five centimetres away from the centre. Cut them out.

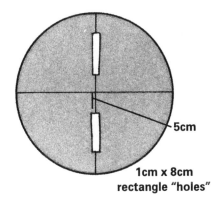

5cm

1cm x 8cm rectangle "holes"

4 Have an adult use the Xacto to slice the straw twice along one-half of its length. Bend the four ''arms'' back to form a propeller. *Firmly* tape and glue the propeller to the circle with the straw centred on the circle. Paint the wheel black on both sides. The wheel is finished.

5 Poke a hole in the centre of one face of the box so the straw fits very snugly. If you make a mistake, just poke a new hole a few centimetres on either side of the first hole *(but not lower)*. Make a mark nine centimetres to the left or right of the hole. Use the cardboard tube to draw a circle whose edge just touches that mark. Cut out the circle. Paint the front of the box black.

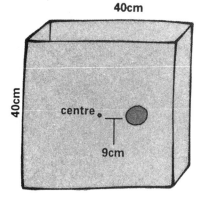

box front

6a If you are using a flashlight, cut a hole in the back of the box in the same place as the round hole in the front, except make this one the same size as the *back* of the flashlight. Slip the cardboard tube

over the front of the flashlight and tape it firmly. Trim the other end of the tube so the flashlight and tube are two centimetres longer than the side of the box. Slip the back of the flashlight into the rear hole, then slide it forward until the tube meets the front hole. Hold it in place with **lots** of tape.

6b If you are using a projector, the idea is the same. But this time make the hole in the back of the box the same size as the one in the front. Connect the two holes with a tube and lots of tape. Position the projector

behind the box so the lens fits snugly into the back hole. Seal with lots of tape.

7 With either method in Step 6, you may paint the inside of the tube white. Temporarily cover the centre hole for the straw, and turn off the lights. Look for light leaks in the box and plug them with tape. Light must only come out the larger hole, **absolutely nowhere else!**

8 This is the creative step. Somehow, you have to position the drill firmly in the box so that the chuck points straight out the centre

front view

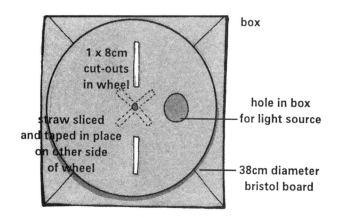

side view (interior)

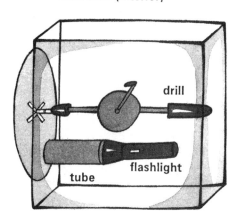

hole. Taping the drill to a smaller box of the right height will work, or to a shelf or cradle at the correct height. Just be sure it doesn't jiggle too much and later pull itself apart.

9 From the outside, insert the drill bit into the chuck and tighten it. Then slip the straw and wheel over the bit. Shorten the straw so the wheel is no more than 1 cm away from the box. (It's O.K. if you have to poke the drill bit through the wheel.) Fasten the straw to the drill with a little tape.

10 Wait until dark, turn on the flashlight, turn off the room lights, and spin the drill. You have just re-invented the flickering light machine, or "stroboscope", or "strobe" for short. Now let's have some fun!

Experiment 1

Ask a friend to stand behind the strobe, and start it spinning in a fully darkened room. Rapidly shake your hand left to right at about

reading distance from your face. Notice that even though you know your hand is moving smoothly (but quickly) from one position to the next, it really looks like it is jerking wildly all over the place. Can you figure out why?

If you look at this same shaking movement of your hand in daylight, the light is steady, so your eyes are getting a steady, smooth image of your hand's motion. But when the strobe is the only source of light, your eyes get only brief stationary flashes of your hand as it quickly and

invisibly changes position in the dark time between flashes. You mind connects the old position with the new position and says "the hand jumped." (If you don't see the jerky motion it means light is leaking into your room, either from your apparatus or elsewhere.)

Some night, go into a room that is only lit up by a TV or fluorescent bulbs and watch your hand wave. Can you figure out why your hand seems to jerk? (That's right, these light sources also flicker, although they flicker faster than the eye can see.)

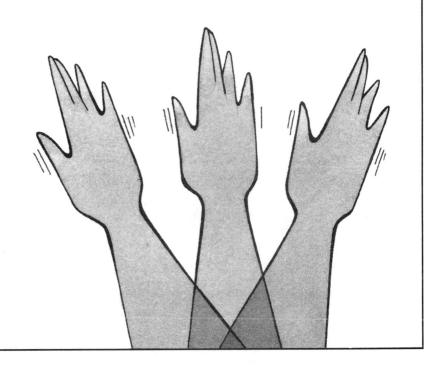

Experiment 2

This next effect seems magical. Poke a clean small hole (about five mm) in the centre of a 12 × 12 cm piece of bristol board. The white side is the front. Attach a strong penlight or flashlight to the back with tape so the beam shines straight out the hole. Gather a bunch of friends, start the strobe, turn on the penlight, and darken the room. Have one friend face the strobe and move the card and penlight left to right and back, making *very fast* changes in direction. Also try different strobe speeds. Very soon, it will appear as if the beam from the penlight passed right off the edge of the card! But how can this be when you firmly attached the pen to the card?

Experiment 1 has the answer. As the diagram shows, the penlight is the path of real motion and that is what you see. However, the card is only seen the few times it is flashed by the strobe. While its image really only lasts a fraction of a second, its afterimage lasts much longer in your eye. Scientists call this visual persistence. So the

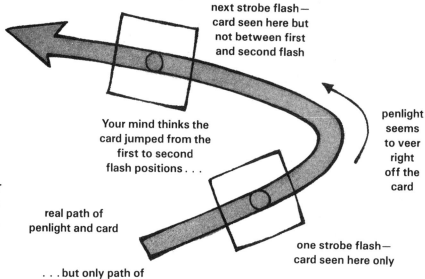

next strobe flash— card seen here but not between first and second flash

Your mind thinks the card jumped from the first to second flash positions . . .

penlight seems to veer right off the card

real path of penlight and card

one strobe flash— card seen here only

. . . but only path of penlight is seen steadily.

afterimage of the card lasts long enough for the real image of the penlight to completely "write over" it and sometimes even beyond. Visual persistence also explains why the moving penlight leaves behind a short "comet's tail."

Experiment 3

To answer the question about wagon wheels in Western movies, you will have to bring a spoked wheel (like the ones on bikes or trikes) and your stroboscope into the same dark room. Turn the bike

upside down, have a friend steadily work the pedal by hand, start the strobe, and turn off the regular lights. *(Keep fingers as far from the spokes as possible.)* Now very slowly and carefully change the speed of your strobe, and watch how the bike's wheel seems to speed up or slow down. Notice that at some strobe speeds the wheel seems to move forward. Other strobe speeds cause it to appear rolling in reverse. And at one very special strobe speed, the wheel seems to be standing perfectly still! Yet all the while the wheel really has been turning forward at

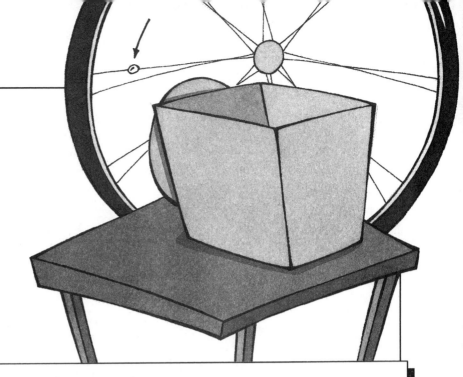

roughly the same speed. Before reading on to find out what is happening, attach a bright bead, or piece of putty or tape to just one of the spokes and repeat everything you did above. Can you figure it out for yourself? (**Hint:** Imagine where that one spoke must be every time the strobe flashes, then think of how your mind is connecting those flashes.)

GUESS
What?

The stroboscope is extremely useful in everyday industry and science whenever it is necessary to watch things that are moving too fast, or to figure out their exact speed. Each day, thousands of mechanics use the strobe to "tune-up" car engines. While the engine is running (at about 850 rounds per minute — rpm) the strobe is triggered by an engine spark at each round. The mechanic points the strobe at the flywheel to see if a special mark always falls in the correct place. If not, she "tweeks" the engine until it

does. Some machines, such as tools, must rotate at exactly the correct speed (if too slow, they don't work; too fast, and they shake and rattle themselves apart). There are professional strobes that can be set to very exact speeds. So, for example, if a tool must rotate at exactly 23 456 rpms, the engineer simply dials that speed into the strobe and plays with the tool speed until its motion is "frozen." You can guess how airplane mechanics measure the speed of propellers or turbines.

Newspapers are printed at

outrageously high speeds. (The *Toronto Star,* for instance, prints 1100 copies a minute). If the press begins damaging papers, it is often impossible to find the problem when the press is stopped. So press operators use strobes to "freeze" the moving machinery to find the problem while it is happening. Scientists use strobes to watch and measure the blindingly fast beating of insect and hummingbird wings (up to 100 flaps per second.) And these are only a few of the many uses of the strobe!

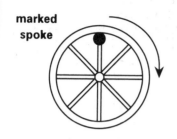

marked spoke

wheel rotating clockwise at a steady speed

This diagram will help with the explanation. Each of the four-frame panels shows how the spinning wheel (at top) would appear when flashed at different strobe speeds. Starting with Panel a, imagine the strobe flashing just a little slower than the speed of the wheel.

In frame 1, the marked spoke is flashed at the top. By the time of the next flash in frame 2, that spoke has spun all the way around and is visible a bit to the right of the last flash. In frame 3, the spoke has again fully spun around and is flashed just past its position in the last

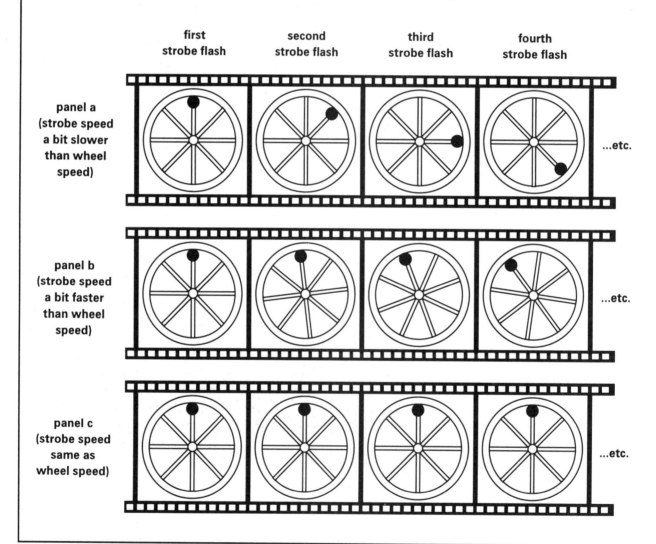

| first strobe flash | second strobe flash | third strobe flash | fourth strobe flash |

panel a (strobe speed a bit slower than wheel speed) ...etc.

panel b (strobe speed a bit faster than wheel speed) ...etc.

panel c (strobe speed same as wheel speed) ...etc.

flash, and so on, and so on. Remember that between flashes the wheel is invisible, so your mind "knits" these frames together and you see a wheel slowly turning clockwise.

In Panel b, the strobe is flashing just a little faster than the wheel. So in frame 1, the spoke is flashed at the top. In frame 2, it is caught just before reaching the top . . . and so on. This time the wheel seems to rotate slowly counterclockwise (backwards).

In Panel c, the strobe's speed exactly matches the wheel's speed. The spokes are always flashed in the same place, so the wheel seems to be stationary.

Can you now begin to see what is happening in old Western movies? It was no accident that the panels in this diagram were drawn to look like film strips. A movie projector is a kind of stroboscope that isn't much more complicated than yours. The main difference is that every time a projector flashes, it projects a slightly different still picture on the screen—like the frames in the diagram. Your mind connects the frames to

SCIENCE
Giants

Harold Eugene "Doc" Edgerton (1903–1990) is known world-wide as the "father" of the strobe. He researched and taught at the Massachusetts Institute of Technology (MIT) for over 60 years. He discovered the strobe totally by accident (the way most brilliant inventors do). In 1927, Doc was really studying the effects of lightning on the way motors perform. His apparatus produced a brilliant short flash exactly each time the motor rotated, and seemed to "freeze" the motion of the motor. He called this lamp a stroboscope and quickly realized its value. Doc devoted his life to refining the strobe and figuring out its many uses. It is now the flash on all cameras, and brings brilliant light to underwater photography. (Jacques-Yves Cousteau's crew called Doc "Papa Flash.") A version of his strobe was used to find many underwater wrecks, including the remains of the *Challenger* space shuttle. He developed over 40 patents and received many scientific and other awards (including a 1940 special effects Oscar). He was loved by all his students and fellow scientists.

© The Harold E. Edgerton 1992 Trust.

produce the illusion of smooth motion. You can figure out the rest from the example. (**Hint**: Imagine filming the wheel rotating just slower or faster than the frames of the projector, or at exactly the same speed.) By the way, you don't see the flashes in a movie because the projector is flickering around 72 times each second, and to most of us, anything faster than about 60 times per second seems to be steady.

As you discovered in Experiment 1, TVs also flicker, so the effect should work there. Can you guess why the effect also happens on the highway at night? That's right—most highway lighting flickers (faster than the eye can see). And why doesn't it happen during the day? Right again—the sun is a very steady source of light!

Experiment 4

Go to a water faucet and turn the water on to form a thin stream. You probably think, along with 99% of the world, that you are looking at a solid column of water being pushed out of the tap. And you guessed it: you're

GUESS
What?

Have you ever coughed and seen your TV's picture disturbed, or watched the illuminated turquoise numbers on a microwave, VCR, or stereo set jump around? If not, stand in front of your TV (turned on, of course) or the illuminated numbers in a completely dark room, and cough. Or

better still, hum as loud as you can, as low as you can, and look for disturbance. Even better is to trill the tip of your tongue against the ridge behind your top front teeth. (Do this very loudly and try different pitches.) If all else fails, crunch on a carrot, melba toast, or peanut brittle and watch the screen or numbers flutter.

You just discovered your own built-in "stroboscope." You know that the TV flickers faster than the eye

can see, but so do those illuminated turquoise numbers. When you cough, hum, trill, or crunch you cause your eyeballs to jiggle in their sockets. The flickering image is then projected on different parts of your retina (as if strobed). The funny thing is that your brain doesn't know that the eyes have moved, so it says "the image must be jiggling". To prove to yourself that it is happening in your head and not out there in the world, tilt your head far over one shoulder and crunch. You will see that the direction of jiggling now lines up with your head (your jaw movements) and not with the illuminated numbers. The numbers sometimes jump when you are doing nothing because your eyes are actually always jiggling, and sometimes they make a bigger-than-normal jump. That's when the numbers jump. Incidentally, the trilling technique was used by early airplane mechanics as a quick way to determine the speed and direction of propellor rotation.

wrong! Bring your strobe to the tap and see what's really happening. That stream is made up of droplets. Strobe at different speeds to make the droplets appear to "freeze" in the air. (If you have a photographer friend, take a picture of the stream at f5.6 for about two seconds or longer using a tripod.) Now find a speed that will make the droplets seem to flow back into the tap! The longer the stream, the better the effect. So, if possible, poke and then plug a hole in a filled two-litre plastic bottle, place it high above your sink, and watch the droplets. Arrange two such bottles so the streams collide and watch that under the strobe. Stick your finger into the stream and watch that with your strobe. Whenever you get a neat effect, take a picture. Strobe other moving things, like the blades of a fan (carefully!), or a friend walking or jumping in front of the strobe. These will make super photos.

If you have access to a video camera, film the whole water experiment. But remember—video, like TV, is also a series of frames, so to get a video recording that resembles what you see, you will have to adjust the speed of the droplets (amount of water) and the speed of the strobe for best results.

GUESS What?

Around the world there are many objects that are associated with miracles. An interesting one is a statue of the Virgin Mary in a cave in Sri Lanka. About 10 years ago people started reporting that they have seen various parts of the statue move. Did the statue *really* move or did the statue only *appear* to move? The reports started after the installation of fluorescent lights. And as you discovered earlier, fluorescent lights flicker! So, to your eye, the whole statue is actually flickering (but too fast to notice). Can you begin to construct a possible explanation? Also remember that your eyes are always jiggling in their sockets.

Two Eyes
ARE
Better Than One

Take a good look at yourself in the mirror. You are looking at a predator! Although today many of us do our hunting in supermarkets, there was a time when all humans actually had to track and capture live prey. This is the main reason we have two eyes pointing forward, as do most predators. Animals that are prey usually have eyes on the sides of the head. Think about deer, rabbits, or starlings. A starling can see completely around itself—from the tip of its beak to the tip of its tail—without moving its head. Such panoramic vision allows it to see a hunting cat approaching from any direction.

The cat, being a predator, has forward-pointing eyes. Unlike the starling, it doesn't have panoramic vision. Without turning its head, and looking straight forward, its field of view is much like ours: roughly half a circle. See for yourself. Look forward and start with both hands straight in front at arm's length. Move them to each side until you can just barely see them in the periphery. They should be roughly opposite each ear. That's your field of view. But most important is the fact that the views of your two eyes overlap a great deal.

Go to a room that is cluttered with many things. Arrange yourself so that something (such as a lamp) is about one metre in front of you. Look at the wall behind it and close one eye. Quickly open it and close the other eye. Do this several times. Did the lamp jump left to right? Of course, it didn't really jump. What you are seeing results from the fact that each eye has a different view of the world, because the two eyes are in different places. With both eyes open, you see only one "picture" of the world. Obviously, the brain must take these two views and fuse them into one. Why did Mother Nature go to such great effort to fuse the two images? Or, we can ask, "What did we gain in place of panoramic vision?" The answer is very simple. We forward-eyed-creatures have the best clue to depth: stereo (3D) vision.

LET'S DO it!

Is stereo vision really such hot stuff? Well, let's see how good you are at judging depth (distance) as a one-eyed, and then as a two-eyed, being.

What You Need and What To Do

1. Ask a friend to hold a sharp pencil in front of you at your arm's length. The pencil should be pointing to your right.

2. You hold another pencil in your right hand pointing toward your friend's pencil. With one eye closed, fairly quickly try to make the pencil points touch (but don't jab each other). Do this several times, without peeking, and have your observer friend estimate how far off you were.

3. Now repeat steps 1 and 2 with *both* eyes open.

This simple experiment tested your ability to judge depth. If you have stereo vision (about eight in one hundred of us don't), you should have been more accurate when you were two-eyed. Let's play with your stereo system some more.

LET'S DO it!

Start by making a stereo viewer—an apparatus that will present separate pictures to each eye. Then you'll look at some stereo pictures.

What You Need

and

What To Do

1 Roll dark construction paper or thin cardboard into two tubes that are 30 centimetres long and eight centimetres in diameter. Tape them along their lengths.

2 Stand them up side-by-side on a tabletop and tape them together only at one end. You should be able to gently pull the other ends apart enough so that each tube can be centred over each eye.

3 Lay the tubes side-by-side flat on the table and place a ruler across them at the taped end. Make a dark line on each tube exactly where the ruler touches them. These marks are the top. You have just made a stereo viewer.

When you hold the untaped ends up to each eye, each one gets a separate view of the world. Now, you need to stick some pictures onto the end of each tube. Pages 95 and 96 show three stereograms. ("Stereo" means three dimensional; "gram" refers to picture.) Each one is actually a pair of pictures—one for the left eye, and one for the right. They were designed to fit your stereo viewer at the taped end.

Photocopy all the stereograms. Cut them out. Notice that each one is marked "L" or "R" for left and right. When you tape

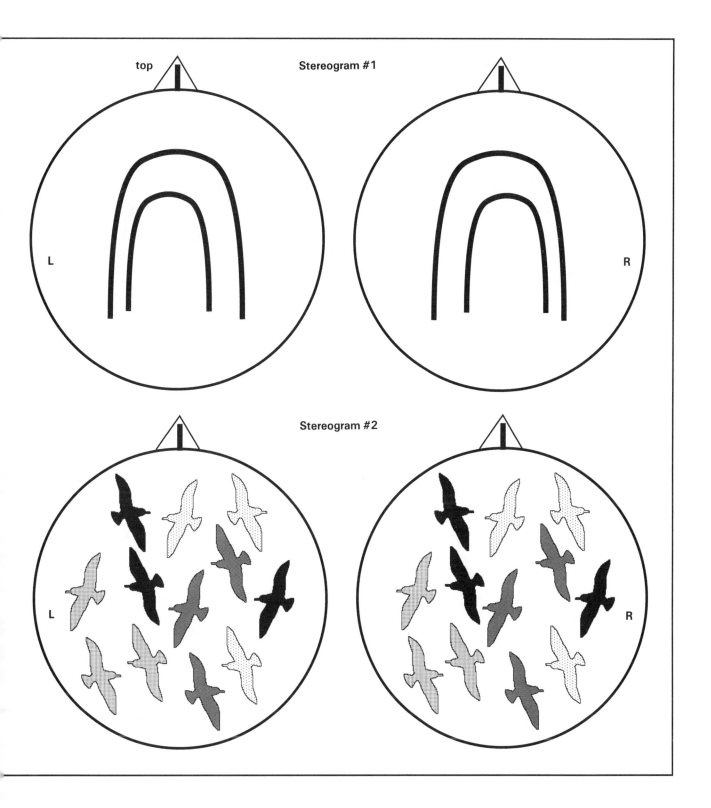

top   Stereogram #1

L   R

Stereogram #2

L   R

Stereogram #3

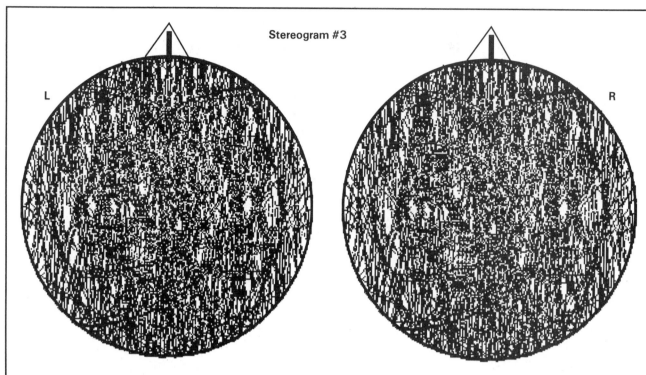

these to the tubes, make sure they go to the correct eyes, and that the top line lines up with the line you drew on the tube. Don't tape them yet, though.

Before you start viewing Stereogram #1, notice how simple it is—just two upside down U-shapes. But look at the smaller U in each half of the stereogram. The one in the left eye is shifted slightly to the left. And the one in the right half is shifted to the right. This copies the views seen by your eyes if you were to look down a real tunnel. (Find something tunnel-like and check it out

for yourself. Look with one eye, then the other, and compare the views.) Now tape your stereograms to the stereo viewer, point it at a bright lightbulb, and see if this tunnel really has depth. The small U-shape should seem farther away than the big one, as if it were the end of the tunnel.

Try drawing your own stereograms, either by hand or using a computer. Imagine, say, what a pyramid looks like from the air. Then draw the views from each eye to produce depth. The main point is to make everything identical in

the two halves except for the parts to be in depth. For something to appear close to you, move those parts in each half *slightly* closer to each other. And do the opposite to make something seem farther away (like the small U-shapes in the tunnel). Be sure to make the shifts tiny. And only move the parts left or right, *not* up or down. Otherwise you'll see double.

Stereogram #2 gives you an idea of why cats need stereo vision. Here is a flock of birds, but the cat can only catch the closest one. You will probably agree that if the cat had only one eye, it would likely starve. (In other words, look at either eye's view and no bird seems closer.) But tape this stereogram to the viewer, and you will quickly get the cat's-eye-view and see which yummy bird is closest. You should be able to figure out how this stereogram was made.

Wild predators that have lost one eye usually don't live very long—partly because their depth judgement is poor and they often miss the prey they want to pounce on. Another reason is the fact that they cannot see prey that is well camouflaged. In Stereogram #3 there is a well-camouflaged zebra. If you were a one-eyed lion, you wouldn't be able to see it. Check it out for yourself. It is quite invisible in either eye's view. Now, tape these to your viewer and see the zebra stand out in 3D. All of a sudden it is easy to see (and maybe just as easy to catch)! This stereogram is simple to make with a computer and a graphics program. Create one half by filling the circle with random lines that look something like tall grass. Duplicate that one, and with an animal-shaped cookie-cutter tool, cut out the animal in each half and move the animals slightly toward each other.

Just for fun, switch the stereograms in your viewer, so each eye sees the wrong half. Before you do that, can you guess what you'll see?

GUESS What?

Your stereo vision is extremely good. In fact, scientists still do not know why. But because it is so good, stereo vision is one of the best ways to detect counterfeit money. When making the plates to print the funny money, the counterfeiter cannot get every single element exactly in the correct place. (That's why our government puts so many little drawings onto each piece of paper money.) Imagine putting a real bill in one side of the stereo viewer and a phony bill in the other. Some of the elements will stand out in depth. But if the bill is real, it should seem flat in the stereo viewer.

Autostereograms

In 1844, Sir David Brewster made a very interesting observation. If you stare at wallpaper that repeats the same pattern, you can get a false impression of depth. Try it out yourself. Find wallpaper that has a constantly repeating pattern like this butterfly paper. The

bigger the wall the better. Now stand one to two metres from the wall and either relax your eyes and stare right through it, or cross your eyes a little. (Don't worry—crossing your eyes *is* healthy.) With time, you should find a position of your eyes where the wall seems either too close or too far from its real position. Keep trying. It is worth the effort. The effect is weird because you know where the wall *really* is. This strange depth effect happens because your brain has taken the two images from your eyes and locked together the wrong elements for the correct depth. So you see the wall at this new depth. Brewster also noticed that if there were tiny imperfections in the printing, such as some elements being misprinted slightly to the left or right, they seemed to pop out in front of or fall behind the wallpaper (the way the birds do in your stereogram).

In 1979, scientists Chris Tyler and Maureen Clarke came up with a way of making stereograms that have both eyes' views in one picture. They called it an autostereogram. It uses dots that are randomly splashed in the picture (sort of like the random lines in your zebra stereogram), but they are moved repeatedly left and right (like Brewster's poorly printed wallpaper pattern and like the butterfly paper). And if you look closely, you can see the repetition. The effect is really neat. Hold the autostereogram at a comfortable reading distance. Now stare beyond the page, or cross your eyes so that the two dots at the top are locked into one. Does anything appear in depth in the dots? (**Hint:** You see it often on St. Valentine's Day.)

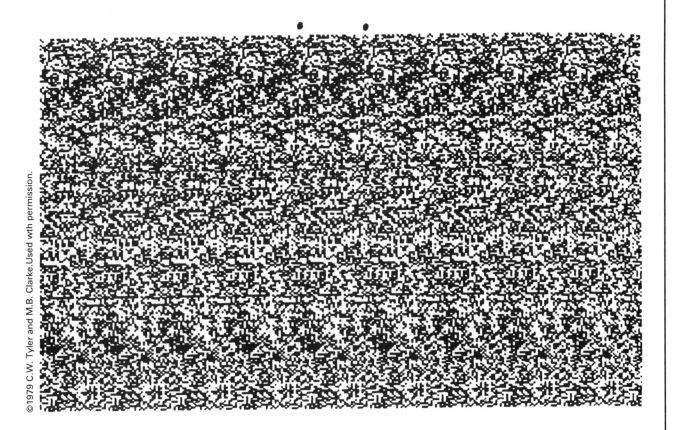

THE
Lone
Rangefinder

In the last experiment, you discovered that stereo vision is perhaps the best way your brain has to figure out how far things are from you. Of course, you must have two eyes to be able to experience and use this method. There is another clue to depth that requires two eyes. Find a place where you can gaze off into the distance. (The moon is a good target.) Close one eye, gently place three fingers on the eyelid, and feel around for your cornea. Now, hold your hand about 20 centimetres in front of your face. With the eye still shut, gaze off into the distance and then at your hand. Repeat this a few times and feel what your covered eye is doing. Imagine a line going from each eye to the thing you are looking at. These are called the "lines of sight." When you look very far away, your lines of sight are nearly parallel. But when you look at something close, your lines of sight point toward each other more strongly. They "converge." Notice also that the covered eye converged even though it couldn't see. Obviously, your brain must know where your eyes are in your head to be able to point the covered eye in the right direction. Scientists think that convergence is another clue to depth.

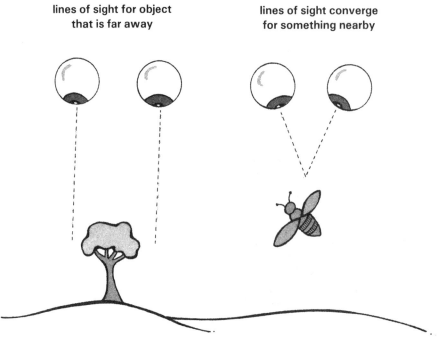

lines of sight for object
that is far away

lines of sight converge
for something nearby

LET'S DO it!

You can use this convergence idea to make an apparatus to measure distance accurately. It is easy to build and use, but accuracy is important. So, read all the instructions first, and if you are unsure about anything, ask your favourite adult to help.

What You Need

a square of stiff cardboard or thin plywood about half a metre by half a metre
a triangle of stiff cardboard or thin plywood about 10 centimetres at the base and half a metre long
scrap cardboard
two pocket mirrors
small nut and bolt (just longer than the thickness of the triangle and the square)
scissors, tape, pencil, and ruler
measuring tape (or 10 metre string with a knot at each metre)

What To Do

1 On the cardboard square, use a pencil and long ruler to draw heavy lines where all the dashed lines on the diagram are. Notice that the short line starts and ends five centimetres from the top-right corner. One long line is the diagonal that runs from the top left to the bottom right. And another one runs parallel to the right side, two-and-a-half centimetres inside of it. On the triangle, draw a line from the tip to the centre of its base.

2 Line up the triangle on top of the square as shown (using the lines on each). Punch, or have an adult drill, a hole *through both*, about three-and-a-half centimetres away from the triangle's base on the centre line. Make a hole that is a snug fit for the bolt. Loosely fasten the triangle onto the square with the nut and bolt. This triangle is now a pivoting arm. (If you are using wood, put one or two washers between the triangle and square so the triangle can swing easily.)

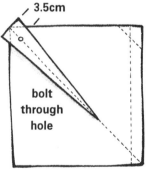

3.5cm

bolt through hole

3 This is the important step. One mirror sits on the line in the top right corner of the square,

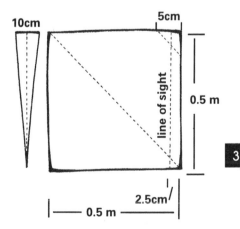

10cm

5cm

line of sight

0.5 m

0.5 m

2.5cm

and another sits on the pivoting triangle. The shiny surfaces of the mirrors face each other. To make this apparatus easy to finish, it is important that the mirrors do not lean forward or backwards too much. (In slightly technical talk, ''the front of both mirrors should be perpendicular to the surface of the large square.'') Make two supports, like the one shown here, out of cardboard scraps. Cut them out and fold along the dotted lines. Tape the long fold to the centre of the back of each mirror. Make sure that the bottom of the mirror and the short fold are level.

4a Positioning Mirror A is easy. Centre it along its dotted line on the square and firmly tape the short fold to the square.

4b Tape Mirror B onto the triangle as close to the bolt as possible. Make it parallel to the line on the triangle. Arrange the mirror so its middle is close to the bolt. Cut a little of the fold on the support to fit around the bolt.

5 Now place your apparatus on something solid in a park or another safe area, so that you have a clear view of things that are far and near. Using one eye, aim the line of sight at something far away, like a tree. Arrange your apparatus so that some of the tree's trunk is above Mirror A.

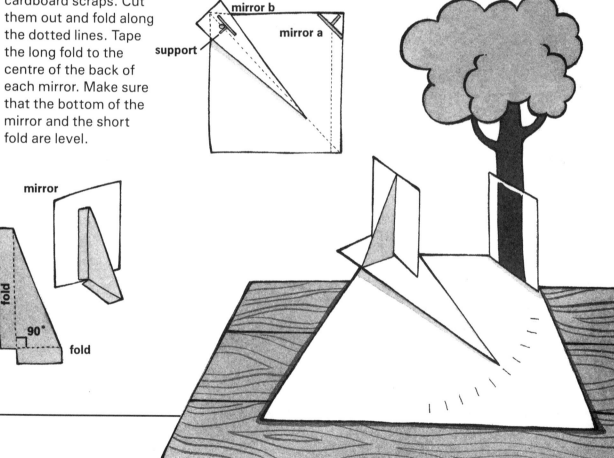

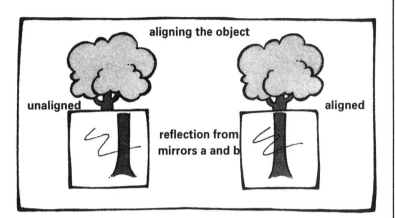

aligning the object

unaligned

aligned

reflection from mirrors a and b

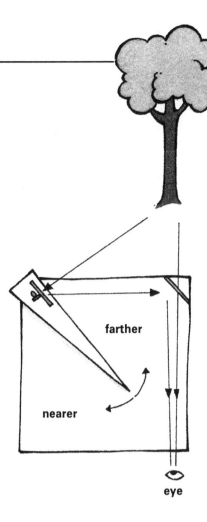

farther

nearer

eye

6 Now gently swing the arm so that the image of the lower part of the trunk lines up with its real top half. (The image of the tree is reflecting off Mirror B, then off Mirror A, and then into your eye.) The diagram shows which way to swing the arm for different distances. When the image and the target are aligned,

freeze! With your measuring tape, carefully measure the distance of the tree from Mirror A. Now immediately run back and place a dark dot where the tip of the triangle is on the square and beside it write its distance. Make other measurements (it's really called calibration) until you have measured and marked several distances from 1 to 200 metres. Now, whenever you want to know how far away something is, all you have to do is haul out your rangefinder, line up the two images, and you will know exactly how far it is. (That's what all the calibration was about.)

A rangefinder is one of the oldest distance-measuring devices around. But it is still used today in many cameras, and by surveyors. Notice that the method is, in fact, very similar to the way scientists think the convergence of our eyes

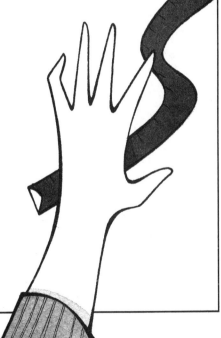

works. For each distance, the eyes—or the mirrors of your rangefinder—have one special convergence. But also notice that, as the object becomes more distant, your marks on the rangefinder are closer together. In other words, distance measurement becomes more difficult, and sloppier. That's also true for the eyes. The solution? Well, for rangefinders, just make them bigger. (If you want to, just multiply all the numbers on the diagrams by two or four or whatever. The important thing is to separate the mirrors as much as possible.) But for us humans that is not a solution because our eyes are fixed in our heads. This explains why convergence, as a clue to distance, only works at close distances. Fortunately, the brain uses many other clues.

SCIENCE
Giants

In the late 1800s, an 18-month-old girl was struck with a disease called scarlet fever. It left her totally and permanently deaf and blind. In the next few years, young Helen Keller became extremely violent, and communicated only with wild grunts and groans, and "crazy" gestures. This isn't at all surprising, since she lost her two most important senses (for communicating) at a stage when her young brain should be going through its most important learning stages. But luckily for her, a teacher named Anne Sullivan thought to reach Helen's mind using the sense of touch.

Anne herself had been nearly blinded from an infection early in childhood. By her early teens, several successful operations had restored much of her sight. However, by that time she had been taught the manual (touch) alphabet. She taught this alphabet to Helen, spelling words into one of her hands while Helen touched things with the other. Eventually, Helen made the connection between the words and their objects, and rapidly began to learn and communicate. Though still blind and deaf, Helen went on to attend university, accompanied by Science Giant Anne Sullivan, who translated lectures into the touch language that Helen understood.

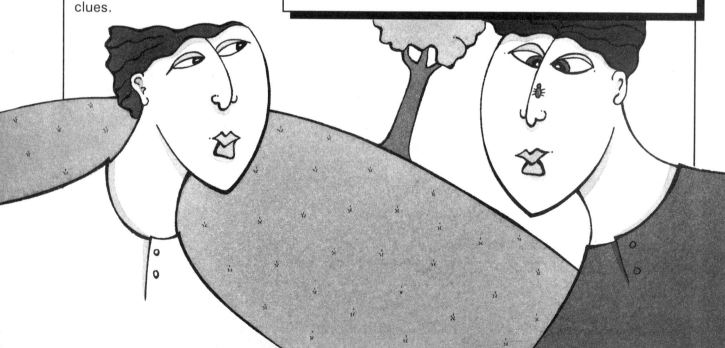

HUMAN
Time Machine

Albert Einstein proved that the speed of time can be changed. But the average person cannot speed up or slow down real time noticeably. (You'd need two synchronized atomic clocks, a rather expensive spacecraft, and a friendly space agency to launch and retrieve it!)

However, the speed of time in your own visual system is always changing. You think the change is a real one out there in the world, but it is actually happening inside you. For example, have you ever noticed what happens when street lights turn on? The lights at the intersections seem to come on just before the other street lights, and the lights seem to turn on in sequence away from you. In other words, the closest comes on first, then the rest in order. Most people think that is

what's really happening. Guess what—*they all come on at* **exactly** *the same time!*

They seem to come on at different times because of a very simple law: the dimmer the light, the longer it takes the signal to reach the brain from the retina. Signals from the brightest lights reach the

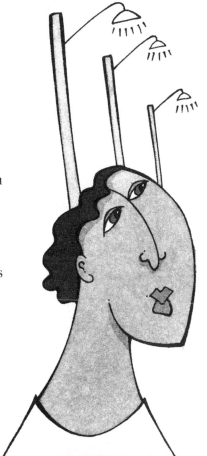

brain the fastest, and the change in time can be large. For example, imagine looking at a race car zooming while you are wearing sunglasses with the left lens (filter) missing. The brain actually receives the image from the filtered right eye about one-tenth of a second later than from the unfiltered left eye. So, the filtered right eye is actually seeing in the past. A tenth of a second does not sound like much, but that's about how long it took the speedier image to get to the brain. In other words, that filter over the right eye *doubled the time of arrival at the brain!* A doubling is a lot. Before we go further, just remember that light isn't being slowed down by the filter. *The signal going to the brain is slowed.* Let's do an experiment, then we'll come back to this idea.

LET'S DO it!

Without an expensive race car or spacecraft, you can still really slow down time.

What You Need

at least one friend/assistant and an adult to supervise
pendulum (for example, a bright tennis ball tied or glued to a long string at least one metre long)
filter (such as dark sunglasses held over one eye or worn normally with one lens poked out; the darker the better but you still must be able to see through it)

What To Do

1 Find a wall with a textured surface (like wallpaper). Attach the pendulum from a high point, such as a solid ceiling fixture, about one metre from the wall.

2 Stand directly facing the wall with the ball at least two metres away from you. Have your assistant start the pendulum on a wide swing from your left to right, making sure the swing is perfectly flat, not circular. Looking with both eyes open, make sure that the ball's path really is flat.

3 Put the dark filter in front of your right eye, and watch with both eyes for a while. Your assistant may have to restart the flat swing. (The effect is stronger if you look at the wall instead of the ball.)

Does the ball's path still seem flat? Probably not. Instead, it looks closer to you when swinging to the right, and farther when swinging to the left. This impression is called an ellipse. Why does a simple filter have this great an effect? The first thing you should observe is that the distance of the ball from you depends on the direction it is moving. Right seems closer; left seems farther. (It also only works with two eyes.

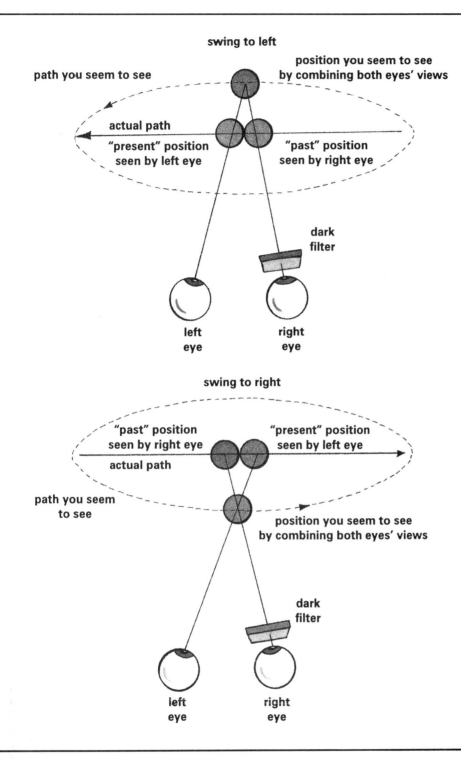

swing to left

position you seem to see
by combining both eyes' views

path you seem to see

actual path

"present" position
seen by left eye

"past" position
seen by right eye

dark
filter

left
eye

right
eye

swing to right

"past" position
seen by right eye

"present" position
seen by left eye

actual path

path you seem
to see

position you seem to see
by combining both eyes' views

dark
filter

left
eye

right
eye

Go ahead and try it with either eye only.)

You know that the filtered right eye is seeing in the past. So, for example, as the ball swings to the left, the brain receives the "present" position of the ball from the left eye, but receives the old "past" position of the ball from the filtered right eye. Think about it. These two images are exactly like a stereogram—only, this one is moving! When the brain combines the two different images into one, it assumes that the ball must actually be farther away than it really is. And that's what you see! When it swings to the right, the ball appears closer than it really is. The faster the ball moves, the greater this depth effect. Stop the ball and there is no depth effect because, while the right is still delayed, both images are in the same place. That's why it seems to make an ellipse shape. In mid-swing the ball is travelling the fastest, and at each end of the swing, the ball actually stops for a moment. Put the filter over the left eye and observe. But before you do that, can you predict what will happen? That's right! Everything will be reversed!

LET'S DO it Again!

The effect you just experienced is called the Pulfrich (PULL-frick) effect. The Science Giant box explains why. To experiment further, try using several filters of different intensities.

What You Need and What To Do

1. Find as many filters of different intensities as you can. Doubling-up two of the same filter will double the darkness.

2. Rank the filters from darkest to lightest and number them in order. Find a differently-coloured pencil crayon for each filter.

3. Tape or glue a pencil to the far end of a metrestick so it points straight up. Find a piece of wood or cardboard that is longer and wider than the metrestick. Place pins on both sides of the metrestick so that it can slide easily back and forth.

4. Align the metrestick so the pencil points exactly underneath the pendulum when it is at rest. The opposite end should be in front of you as you face the pendulum. Mark on the board where your end of the stick sits, and place a zero beside that mark. This is the actual position of the pendulum.

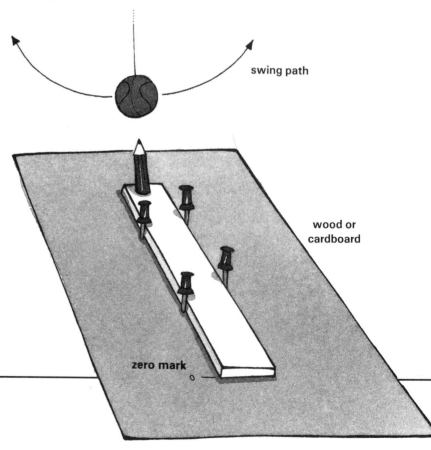

swing path

wood or cardboard

zero mark

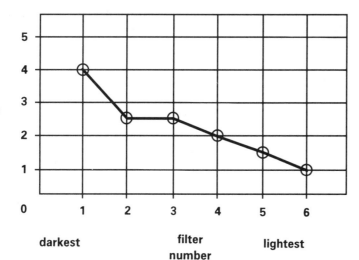

average distance (in cm)

darkest   filter number   lightest

SCIENCE Giants

This pendulum effect was first described and explained in 1922 by the German physicist Karl Pulfrich, *who was blind in one eye!* He never experienced the effect, because it requires two normal eyes and normal stereo vision. Instead, Karl came up with the explanation using only mathematics and, without a doubt, a very rich imagination!

 5 Begin with the darkest filter over your favourite eye, and start the pendulum swinging perfectly flatly.

6 Slide the stick so that the pencil points to where the pendulum seems to be while it is swinging. When you are satisfied, mark with the correct coloured pencil where your end of the stick is. Do this three times for the forward swing, and three times for the backward swing.

7 Slide the stick out of the way, and now use it to measure the distance of each of the six marks from the zero line. Take their average. (Add them up and divide by six).

8 Repeat steps 5–7 with the next lighter filter, until you have tested all the filters.

Make a graph like this one and mark a dot for each of your observations. For example, in this graph, the darkest filter was called #1 and on average the stick was set 3 cm away from zero. With the next filter (#2), the stick was set 1.5 cm away from zero . . . and so on. (Your numbers will probably be different from these mainly because your filters are probably very different.) You'll likely find that the line connecting the dots is high on the left and slopes down to the right. This means that the Pulfrich effect lessened as the filter got lighter. Put another way, dark filters slow the signal to the brain more than light filters do.

If you don't experience the Pulfrich effect, it may be because your filter isn't dark enough. Or you might be one of the many people who are stereoblind. This would mean you have trouble forming one image from the two presented by your eyes and can't "pull-out" the depth. Check to see if you also can't see depth in the stereograms a few pages back.

Next time you travel in a car, bus, or train, take along your sunglasses. Look out the right window with the right eye filtered and notice how things appear closer than they really are. Compare that with the left eye filtered, where everything seems farther than it really is. That's right—it is the Pulfrich effect. Do the same thing while watching your favourite movie. If anyone asks what you're doing, just say you're taking an in-depth look at the past and present!

GUESS
What?

Have you ever watched jets landing at an airport and noticed how the big jumbo jets, like 747s, seem to take forever—almost as if they were hanging in the air—but the smaller jets seem to approach much more quickly? Believe it or not, commercial jetliners, large or small, in the same situation all land at almost identical speeds. This points out a very basic law in vision: the speed something appears to be moving at depends on its size. Large things seem to lumber along, while tiny things seem to zip about. This effect might explain why there is such an unusually great number of car accidents at railway crossings in clear, broad daylight, involving normal, sober people. It was once thought that these people were risk-takers or suicidal. Scientists now think that most accidents are caused by the driver's serious underestimation of the huge locomotive's speed.

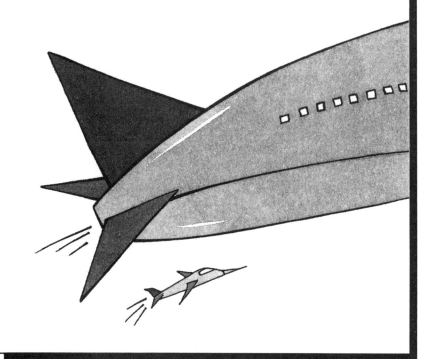

Glossary

(Does not include the terms defined on pages 10–13 and 56–62.)

acoustic reflex An automatic tightening of your ossicles that produces temporary deafness.

acuity The smallest visible distance between two objects.

borborygmus The loud rumbling and growling that comes from your abdomen.

convergence The position of your eyes as they turn inward when looking at something.

diaphragm The powerful muscular membrane that separates your chest cavity from your abdomen.

Doppler Effect The drop in frequency as a sound source zooms past you. You hear a drop in pitch.

epiglottis The flap just behind the tongue that prevents food and liquids from entering the lungs when you swallow.

Escherichia coli A type of bacteria found in your intestines that helps you digest your food.

esophagus The tube connecting your throat to your stomach.

field of view The amount of space in all directions that you can see with both eyes open.

harmonics The many frequencies produced by most sound sources which we hear as a single sound. They are also called overtones. Different instruments produce different sets of harmonics.

hertz (Hz) The unit of measurement for frequency. Two hundred vibrations per second is 200 Hz.

infrared Energy that is beyond the red end of the light spectrum, and is invisible to humans. We feel it as heat.

infrasonic Sound waves that humans cannot hear (below 20 Hz).

Mach Unit for the speed of sound in air. Mach 1 is one times the speed of sound (1200 km/h), Mach 2 is twice . ... and so on.

OptoKinetic Nystagmus (OKN) This is a reflexive jerking of the eyes that takes place whenever a large part of your field of view moves.

panoramic vision The huge field of view that creatures with side-mounted eyes have.

parabola A U-shaped curve that has a focal point. Parallel rays travelling into the parabola all cross this focal point.

photoreceptor A cell in the retina designed to change light energy into electrical signals. Humans have two types: rods and cones.

rangefinder An apparatus that uses a reflected image and the direct image of an object to measure the object's distance from you.

resonant frequency The special frequency that an object can be caused to naturally vibrate.

stereo vision The perception of the depth (distance) dimension by combining the slightly different views seen by the two eyes.

stereogram   A pair of pictures, copying the views seen by each eye, that when seen in a stereo viewer produces an impression of depth.

stroboscope   A device that produces bright, crisp flashes of light.

timbre   The quality of a sound that makes various instruments playing the same note sound different. It results from the unique set of harmonics each instrument produces.

ultrasonic   Sound waves (above 20 000 Hz) that humans cannot hear.

ultraviolet   Energy that is beyond the blue end of the light spectrum and invisible to humans.

uvula   The "punching bag" flap easily seen hanging down at the back of the mouth.

visual persistence   Images that last longer than the actual duration of the image itself. Visual persistence is partly caused by the fact that signals take time to travel through the visual system.